A PENTECOST OF FINCHES

New and Selected Poems

A PENTECOST
OF FINCHES

New and Selected Poems

Robert Siegel

PARACLETE PRESS
BREWSTER, MASSACHUSETTS

Pentecost of Finches: New and Selected Poems

2006 First Printing

Text copyright © 2006 by Robert Siegel

Frontispiece etching, "Untitled," copyright © 1983, 2005 by Lenaye
   Siegel-Hudock

ISBN 1-55725-430-3

Library of Congress Cataloging-in-Publication Data

Siegel, Robert, 1939-
   A Pentecost of finches : new and selected poems / Robert Siegel.
      p. cm.
   ISBN 1-55725-430-3
   I. Title.
   PS3569.I382P46 2006
   811'.54–dc22   2005026916

10 9 8 7 6 5 4 3 2 1

Published by Paraclete Press
Brewster, Massachusetts
www.paracletepress.com

Printed in the United States of America

FOR ANN

dear
image of that beauty and grace
who loves us with a human face.

CONTENTS

NEW POEMS

SELECTED POEMS

ix

ACKNOWLEDGMENTS

I am grateful to the following journals and anthologies in which some of the poems were first published: *The Atlantic:* "Air Field," as "Hanscom Air Field," "The Very First Dream of Morning"; *Poetry:* "A Bear," "Ego," "A Lady Who Lov'd a Swine," "Hog Heaven," "Bull"; *Prairie Schooner:* "Christmas Eve," "Peonies," "Fireworks"; *New England Review:* "Submariner," "Now They Stand Still"; *Georgia Review:* "Grandfather Chance"; *The Cream City Review:* "Swimming Snake," "Mussel," "Slug"; *Midwest Quarterly:* "Simple Simon"; *The Beloit Poetry Journal:* "Sow's Ear"; *Verse:* "Tiger"; *Books & Culture:* "Going On," "Daddy Long Legs," "The Serpent Speaks"; *Granite:* "Poet"; "Hunting in Widener Library," "Voice of Many Waters"; *Midland Review:* "Grendel," as "Sasquatch"; *Image:* "Carrying the Father," "Alligator," "Evening Wolves," "Rat," "Snail," "Seer"; *Cresset:* "Deer Tick," "The Surgeon After Hours," "How to Catch a Poem," "Wings," as "Raphael"; *Sow's Ear:* "Lobo"; *The Humanist:* "Sheep at Nightfall" as "Sheep"; *First Things:* "Spider"; *America :* "The Hunt," "Aubade," as "Morning Song"; *The Christian Century:* "Giant Panda"; *For the Time Being:* "Morning's at Seven"; *The Chicago Tribune*

Magazine: "Gettysburg: The Wheatfield"; *Your Own Poets:* "The Shroud"; *Kodon:* "Shopping Together"; *Made for Each Other:* "A Song of Praises"; *From The Tongue of the Crow: Wisconsin Review Anthology:* "The Hunter"; *Stories for the Christian Year:* "A Colt, the Foal of an Ass"; *Sightseers into Pilgrims:* "Snakesong"; *Poems for a Small Planet: Contemporary American Nature Poetry:* "Turtles," "Silverfish"; *Contemporary Poetry of New England:* "Spring Peepers."

I am grateful to the publishers of my previous books represented here, *The Beasts & the Elders, In A Pig's Eye,* and *The Waters Under the Earth,* for permissions granted and assignment of copyrights. I am grateful as well to the University of Wisconsin-Milwaukee for sabbatical and other grants, and to Dartmouth College, the Ingram Merrill Foundation, and the National Endowment for the Arts for poetry fellowships, all of which supported the work over time.

I wish to thank especially Jeanne Murray Walker for her wise and generous advice in this process. Likewise I want to thank George Young and my wife, Ann, for their invaluable suggestions along the way. Last, I thank my editor, Lil Copan, for her encouragement and marvelous patience, as well as my publisher, Lillian Miao; Jon Sweeney; Sister Mercy; and all the staff at Paraclete Press.

NEW POEMS

ONE

Climbing out of the lake,
  I first notice him
on the other side of the pier,
  swimming, his elegant head
and eye on a level with mine.

Yellow and dark green stripes
  rise to a flittering red
tongue where he glides easily
  as a thought over water
toward the tall pickerel weeds.

Each striped blade mirrors
  his long inquiring neck
while free of the dust at last,
  at his ancient altitude,
he swims, tasting the air

with the red fire of his tongue.
  The frogs have all submerged,
leaving the burning lake
  a blank page of light
for his brilliant, flowing script—

for the elusive subtleties
  of his complicated tale
and dazzling nemesis.
  Drying off on the dock,
I smell the lake on my skin,

an odor that insinuates
  his dark evolving thesis,
his rolling, eloquent S
  that shrinks on the floor of light
to lose itself in the shadows
  of the striped pickerel weeds.

Old familiar, breathing through a reed
under the green fen,
lurker from a watery cave where flames die,
hissing your name,
Feond, Ferly, Marsh-stalker,

How often have we filed tooth and nail, shaved
a witch-knotted pelt,
only to find your fangs glittering over
a moonscape of self.

You cling, an overcoat, a cape, a Frankenstein's
monster, forsworn,
hunched moon we bring all our children,
born and unborn,

from that Transylvania of the soul where
Dracula's not dead.
Though a stake's hammered through, his heart
twitches at the crossroad

while a fool flush with victory pauses where
weird sisters sing
what a little thing it is to kill
the anointed king.

When the full moon draws a chalk circle,
your lingering howl
floats from the burning meadhall. We follow
an uncertain trail

of dribble from your severed arm, avoid
each other's eye,
not knowing which will enter the stinking pool, face
your drooling dam,

and bring up your head that stares witless from
the whites of its eyes,
its ears stone to the voice in the reeds
murmuring prophecies

of the undying dragon and unending wars.

DEER TICK

. . . *no larger than the period at the end of this sentence.*
                                   —*The* Milwaukee Journal Sentinel

No larger than a period I scramble
among the sequoia of your armhairs
unable to decide in this vast wilderness
where to drill for the life-giving well
the water of life, the warm blood.
For I am sick unto death: in my abdomen

the spirochete turns its deadly corkscrew
which I must shortly confess to the stream
pulsing from your dark red heart,
setting at liberty this ghostly germ
large in the deer's glazed eye
and the mouse's tremble.

I have carried it for generations
like a secret so long in the family
no one remembers where it came from,
like a small hiatus in the genetic code,
or a choice, an act, a curse
set loose in the wilderness of youth:

a prodigal gone to a foreign city to prosper
and return with mercenaries and fire.
I carry this secret like the memory of a war,
of an evaporated nation, of a people
turned to haze on the horizon
that recedes as you drive toward it, an elusive

virus that lies dormant
and then imitates every other plague
as it maneuvers toward the final crisis:
This mist at the corner of your eye
this telltale shape that one day will fall
over your shoulder into the morning mirror.

This voice that comes in the pit of night
when all the others are still
and tells you precisely what you fear
what you cannot shrug off, repeating itself
on smaller and smaller tapes:
Yes, let me tell you, I will tell you
gladly. Here, I put my mouth closer,
so close I won't need to whisper.

TIGER

Like these shadows
I flow in and out of myself.
In a stand of bamboo, I am invisible
until my mouth flashes a rose
and another lies under my claws.

In the green shade I flow with ambiguities.
The birds above debate my arrival
until I take shape at the center,
absolutely necessary, giving form
to the redundancy of leaves,
to the panicked circuses of monkeys.

My voice, a low engine turning over,
guttering, has a certain resonance,
vibrates through every root, climbs through
the cilia of insect-eating plants,
travels along the vines
and through the toppling kingdom of the ant.

I drag my victim from the waterhole—
the cow, the zebra, the wildebeeste—
and feast among my retinue, who boast
and chatter of my deeds at a respectful distance.
I am regal and lazy in my eating,
tolerant, when full, of those paying court,

hyena, jackal, and other politicians,
each suing for bones—his own and the other's—
while I perform my ablutions in public
like Louis XIV, no least fretting or cleansing
of my fur beneath the scruple of each eye.

You might say it is my finishing school—
not the least thing lost on those around me
of how they should behave toward one another.
You might say my feasting establishes order
that ripples out in circles

to the least and frailest link in my kingdom.
Even the table I lay is splendid
and instructive—glistering, colorful,
spread out in the sun—
creating symmetry, perfection, a hush
that follows on my velvet tread.

Llama

I hold my head up, surprised by a white peak
you are at the wrong altitude to see.
My body floats in a graceful rhythm under it
but my head always maintains its simple poise.
I am the soft white of wool and yet inside
burns the impossible white of sun
on a distant snowfield no one has ascended
except my ancestor from Macchu Picchu,
a scapegoat, a messenger, an aspiration
the ancient Incas unfurled
to the severe deity of snow:
a banner, a dignity, a throne, a power.

Should you be lucky enough to ride my back
on a saddle of many-colored wools,
do not engage me in idle conversation.
Note how each hoof picks an invisible home
on the vertical rocks. All you can do is hug
the moving question-mark of my neck
as we pass over the stark canyons
on bridges of snow, the clouds
floating halfway down, the bells
on my harness accompanying us like birds.

No need to tether me at night, and at dawn
do not approach me directly or look in my eye
for I spit with notorious accuracy,
an unsavory comment on your indelicacy.

Notice how we have wound about these peaks,
how the trail has disappeared many times,
the stone crosses marking the unexpected descents,
the thinning of the ether,
the great gods that burn at night above us
muttering and thundering in their sleep.
The streams merely gurgle now or fall like mists
across the vastness.

Your fingers turn blue outside of the serape.
You talk in your sleep of your lover, oxygen.
I listen with the silver ear of the moon all night
and bend and breathe a little warmth on your face.

When we reach the ice palace, the great snow field,
the flashing caves where the rainbow hums
in the green wall and meet the naked one
warmed by his own meditation, clothed
in the moss of starry speculations, he'll open
to you the first step, impossible yet simple,
of the journey you think you have completed
but which, in fact, you are only now beginning.

GIANT PANDA

In the white mist of morning I find my place,
a square of the sun where I can balance

and chew the shoots, their green light in my mouth.
I sit, my footpads shiny, taking in the dim

sweet music of existence. On the mountain
when the enlightened one came holding the flower,

Kashya smiled. So it has ever been
as I move, myopic, from blossom to blossom.

I am the bear who sees your original face
a hundred years before you were born.

I sit, the world circling about me,
holding the secret between tongue and palate,

the sweetness of nothing, above which
the mind shimmers like a forest of silks.

for Ihab and Sally Hassan

INCHWORM

I never feel quite all together.
Part of me leaves before I've gotten here,
abstracted as I am by numbers
by that invisible world where one and one equal one
by the calculus, pebble on pebble,
by measurement and all extrapolation
that give me a past and future
and mean I'll arch over the present.

When I come to the end of your finger I reach out
finding nothing, open to it, quivering,
with my little pod feet
swaying back and forth,
not able to make the leap,
and turn back on myself and hump back down
to the thin forest of hairs on your arm.

I am always in two places
the past and the future, never wholly present,
lost in repeated calculations
the stars taught me: a straight line between two
points,
that one and one equal one and one,
the moments dropping like pebbles in a pool.

I slide and fatten like the worm
of the Nile in the spring
leaving measurement where I pass
in mud and stone. The pyramid of Cheops
and all such monuments began
as I counted myself over and over along a stick.

I am of two minds moving out of sync—
when one's in action, the other's resting,
and so I never come to a conclusion
though we move in the same direction
by separate steps, by little omegas,
yet neither end comes ever to an end.

Though I am certain of nothing
except the arch I make for light to pass under
in a space I've measured again and again
in seconds and particles and waves,
when you put me on a green leaf
I blend in and am comforted
and forget for a while definition
in a wilderness of foliage, annihilating
all that's made to a green thought
that resolves the two halves of my brain
until at last with the shimmering leaves
I flow upward.

Lo, I am a milk machine, my udder
swells like a sail promising a sea of milk.
The steel cans huddle and clink like an army
waiting for food, waiting for me to sing
in the agony of delivery.
                            Lo,
they listen as I bring up my cud from the darkness
and mournfully chew the green memory of fields
I have never grazed, sun I have never glowed in
like one of Van Kuyp's bovine vessels of light
or a sheet on washday, a homely angel
pronouncing every beast good.

Instead I stand and chafe against these stainless
steel bars, fixed to this one spot while
the fluorescent lighting numbs me with its buzz
of a thousand absent flies. The floor is hard,
antiseptic, and my ragged wheels of dung
float off on a conveyor belt while the golden arc
of my urine is hosed away by ammoniac sensors.

My hide glistens from two sanitary scrubs
a day, but my poor bones, square as a map
of the United States, rust in this narrow cell
while the Mexico of my udder swells and seethes.
Even the little tubes that suck and suck
with rubber mouths are dead on my teats like a glove.

I feed, give milk, and drool.
My eyes are dull, filled with a white sleep,
my ears with the irritant of the radio turned up
to churn my stomachs faster.

When I was blue, cauled, unlicked, they pulled me
from my mother, my four feet roped together,
to bawl in a whitewashed cubicle with a rubber teat.

In this long blue twilight I sink into beastly patience
like all my kind who grieve, having lost their world—
the earth, violent and sweet to eye and ear,
hide, nose, and mouth—
to live fixed, idiotic, as if nailed to a tree.

I give some thousands of gallons of milk and then,
after no life but this blue worrying light,
come through a fast-food window ten to a pound.

I ask you,
what have I ever done to deserve it
but reveal a contentment you cannot stand?

When it is cold
when the air cracks like a hundred-year-old tree
when there is the thinnest nothing
and the lake is clear and hard as the moon,
I come forth and sniff the air,
my fur around me sleek as thought.
I scent and scent and then
give the moon back to the moon in one long O,
give the ice to the moon and the yawning lake
and the stiff black fur of the trees,
and my O fills the sky
till the others come
low, loping, yittering and yelling back,
lashing the air with their quick tongues
like a mob coming toward the palace,
like the tongues of a million unmarked graves,
like ten-thousand sirens in a thousand cities,
the gray, the silver, and the white with black foot.
We sit in council,
chasing the moon on its way,
supporting the sky, rounding out its hollow,
and our music is murder over the hills,
cold tongues on your back,
the sharp tooth at your throat,
and slaver glittering over your stiff eyes.
You, lying in the hollow,
you, turning in the cold bed, afraid to drop
down into the black lair of sleep

with its ten-hundred-million pleading mouths
and its insistent hungers,
you, before whom the electric eye flickers in the dark,
shrinks to a pinpoint, and goes out
after dropping at your feet a hundred corpses
from a dozen different countries,
each with a story, each with a vision
at which you can only stare without speaking
as they stalk you on lupine foot.

NIGHTCRAWLER

What I love I take whole into my mouth
and pass through it as it passes through me.
It is dark and wet and made of everything that has
ever been.

I am blind and buried in it, yet it goes on
forever, in one silent mouthing, an endless aria.
I drink it in, and weep it, sliding moistly through it,

loosening it, even as it welcomes me, bringing the sky
down into it. I push, then drag
my whole self like a long afterthought,

writing a strange line looping in mystery,
now and then following the spoor of the others
through tunnels smooth with sorrow toward the light.

In the dark, broken by faint wormholes of light,
when the cool dew settles on us in the air,
we slide out into the naked element,

and find each other, wrap around the other
tightly. In that moment, anchored
to the ground and to each other in the heavens,

we are positive and negative poles,
electricity from earth to sky and back,
having the long speechless speech all flesh desires,

vulnerable as all flesh, no bone or beak to shield us,
blind, a naked want that has finally joined another
to a fullness, to a moment of no-time,

when all the echoes shaking the ground return in one
                                        sweet vibration
as if the earth itself would leap up and take form,
as if all life that has passed through us

would stand together and tremble into shape,
and stone itself, the rock keeping mute its secret,
would finally confess light, light,

and begin a slow and luminous dance of forms.

SPIDER

But rather seek
Our own good from ourselves and from our own
Live to ourselves, though in this vast recess
Free, and to none accountable.
                    —Mammon in Paradise Lost

ZZ. The fly is at the sill. ZZ ZZ.
I am silent, riding the center
of my web, the intricacy of my thought
spelled out like the stars and the bonds between them.
ZZ ZZ ZZ.
My feet make no noise as I dance to the edge

of my galaxy, this gossamer star-net that catches
the gray light filtering through the window.
Here at the edge of the void through which I
extend myself, I listen to the fat
stumbler, him of the single idea
that the glass will suddenly dissolve, this one

who crawls upward on gluey feet and flails
stubby wings until he plummets, his eyes
rotating, twin red turrets. He tries and sputters
tries and fails again. Satisfied,
I return to the tensile center, all my wits
sharpened to wait. For have I not written

out my thoughts to the gods?—I, who fell
from heaven on a single strand,
unraveling myself, and found this eminence
to attach to—and then that—and that—
in the void, in the whispering chaos,
and, groundless, swung myself through the night,

launched out on the rope of myself to meet
the other like an echo of myself,
trailing the strong cord of my being
in parallel dodecagonals until
the pattern of my soul was laid out. Then
the great square of day shone dim as the white

eye of the sun climbed up and I saw
the beautiful design
of myself flex silver in all directions.
The small gnats fly to it in admiration
and sing, fascinated, as I weave them into it
and drink their song, my hunger slightly abated.

Now I wait for this sad, black-booted fellow,
this drab swashbuckler thick with the dust
of his fellows who failed before him—
this worn-out singer of song who turns
one eye backward in fear, one forward in desire,
who thinks there is a world outside the glass

of color and open spaces, grown tired of
my twilit world where things silver with thought
and dry up. Let him bluster and crawl!
Soon now, in his last careering search
for a way out of the dark he'll find my net,
a shimmer of moonlight sticking to his wings,

a deadly, impossible music that catches
him mid-air, a symphony that wraps
him round though he saw at it frantically
with his small violin until it silence him—
until he hangs, a note like the others
in this universal score I have composed:

my choral symphony, to which I'll offer up
his small soul in gratitude, that it might swell
larger, ever expanding in this darkness,
until he hangs, a shell as weightless
as if he'd vanished through the glass, transfigured
by the endless contemplation of my being

into my very self, a burned-out satellite,
a dead star. Meanwhile I wait
all night at the center
filled with a sweet surfeit of being,
sensitive to each wave and vibration
along its radii, listening for news
of life stirring at the far-flung edges.

GIRAFFE

Light brown and reticulate yellow, I breathe
the altitude of the cockatoo and python.
The sun falls down me in a ladder and invites

whoever knows what a leaf aims at to climb to the heaven
of green waterfalls and ropey spaces I lean among
like a shambling tower of desires. I am the campanile

ringing the shadows of the hours, a dappled shaft
and burst of light in the forest. My feet move
with the delicacy of waiters carrying a tray of desserts.

My body aches upward: it reveals gravity as the illusion
necessary to form. I am the original ascetic
in the Egyptian oases

tonguing the leaves in voluptuous self-denial,
folding them one by one into a sumptuous chewing
followed by a peristaltic descent of my throat

like an elevator's, lights flashing at every floor,
toward my legs spread firmly against the earth.
My neck is Solomon's strong tower

surrounded by armed men with bucklers,
the air sweet with pomegranates, the tinkling ankles
and brown trembling flanks
of the Queen of Sheba in a yellow net of light.

The giraffes totter onwards, sweet derelicts of heaven.
They do not cry to each other, they have no voice,
their mouths are dumb on the pennybread of heaven.

One is an albino, walking lightning,
an incredible architectural nudity,
the legs and angles we would melt upward into,

the nude ascending a staircase cubed in four dimensions,
all legs and lovely neck like the girl we saw
at fourteen at the mixer in the blue taffeta

and were afraid to dance with,
she moved so slenderly
like air moving in air

a column of sky
the invisible stem of a cloud
that led up to the piled morning of her hair:

the girl who was silent
whose sweet head swayed from leaves to invisible leaves
as she browsed the heavens and we

boys, shoes polished, lurked in the men's room
with hair oil, comb, and the panicked heart
entangling itself the more it tried to escape.

Like a simple idea uniting earth and heaven,
a simple idea marrying stars to the earth,
another dimension we could be beamed up into,

the answer to a question we hardly dared ask,
like Shelley's smile that kindled the universe:
escalator to *that* . . . *that* . . . *that* . . . .

THE SERPENT SPEAKS

Soul: Look on that fire, salvation walks within.
Heart: What theme had Homer but original sin?
                              —Yeats

And three begot the ten thousand things.
                              —Lao Tzu

I am another vine
in the great democracy of vines
part of the complexity that defies explanation
part of the tree you put your back to
alert, but never suspecting.
I am the cold coil around the warm trunk,
I expand
as your lungs, poor rabbits, twitch and swell.
I am a long story with lovely yellows
        and dapples and shades
a beginning, middle, and end that you can get lost in
a sunny patch followed by a shadow
a green dapple and twist, the turn, the unexpected
        reversal.
When you come to the denouement
                and my tail narrows to nothing
you wish to go back to the beginning and start over
where the red lie flickers in the leaves
beneath eyes like mica moons.

It is the old story, the beginning of everything
but really a long divagation and excursus
in which the woman naked and trembling
    complains to the man, weeping over and over
        and his voice rises in sharp jabs
            while all their unborn children listen.

It is something that interrupts the afternoon, the first day,
and history begins and wanders off for millennia
    missing the whole point.

It is these subtle shades on my scales
this maze of intricate lines
that lead back upon themselves in endless recursions
that fascinate you, that lead you endlessly
from my tail into my mouth.
In the moving light of the jungle I am a simple
body-stocking of shadows and weave
under a fritillary of bird cries to a sensuous music
a harmony to all your doings
promising you the ultimate knowledge in my belly
down the dark tube of years:
Light and shadow, light and shadow, the days and nights pass
with increasing speed like stations and their intervals
and you sway holding the strap
the car-lights flickering
wondering whatever was your original destination.

29

When fiction held out its red lie among the roses
you followed it down my dark throat.
It seemed utterly reasonable. Then you were Methuselah
carrying each of his 900 years like a brick on his back
Abraham's wild surmise with a knife
Joseph starving in a hole
and Moses singeing his feet in the wilderness.
Next they hung you from two sticks and slowly
everything grew more dramatic:
Augustine heard the children in the garden
Aquinas fled from the naked peasant
and Columbus woke in a sweat, the voices still singing
of a lost world
of amber waves and alabaster
until Lord Amherst gave his blankets to the Indians
Franklin saw the flashing key
and Washington sold his horse for pasturage
until the utterly reasonable Robespierre offered up his head
Lenin popped from a boxcar
and Einstein gave you the terrible secret
which I had promised,
a man of violins and God.

Now the story has gotten out of hand
as you swarm upon yourselves like maggots
    on a diminishing dung-pile
        and frenzied, move toward the catastrophe
history a string of boxcars
    each a century stuffed to overflowing
        until the last leaps the track.

Meanwhile I who am the truth move
scintillatingly, with grace in my own shadow
telling the story: *There was a man, and a woman. . .*
and the sun rose
and they went on a long journey
and night fell and they did not know where they were.

Such is knowledge, such is the fruit I offered
without the encumbrances of love, without listening
without the tree of fire that burns
below all movement, all shining, the tree below the bones
whose flames reach through the skeleton and hover
just over the fingers

and burn away the forest where the ego
goes crying, alone—one eye balancing the other
bilaterally symmetrical—
of what it has and what it hasn't
until all shapes are shining and
fear falls away shriveling like a black net
and the wisdom of God dances freely before you
and the glowing fruit blushes for the mouth.

I see all clear and can tell you
the end of things, knowing you will not listen,
for my knowledge is cold here in the forest
and you will follow the shifting arabesque
of moonlight on my mica-glint, my scales
moving like the sequins of days, events,
the rise of stocks and the next presidential election
and the price of wheat futures in a drought.

31

So I go on, flowing into my own shape
into the darkness I have made, subservient
(and this is the bitterness beyond all blankness)
at the last to another purpose
　　　which you cannot guess, which rings in these leaves
like the harps and fiddles of insects too high
for your range of hearing—a music which drives me
into the narrowing circle I have made
tail in mouth, swallowing until

　　　　　　　　　　　　I vanish
and everything in this circle vanishes with me.

TWO

Portraits

A NOTABLE FAILURE

He never went abroad to broaden him
and though he learned to read, he did not write
anything worth saving. Once, at a whim,
he scribbled something they hadn't gotten right

in the sand and erased it. Few could know
whether to credit any of the vulgar rumors
surrounding his birth in a shed. There were low
whispers and a gap of thirty years.

Then more rumors trickled through the countryside
about the artisan's son turned wonderworker:
probably a charlatan—blasphemer to be sure. Wide-eyed,
some claimed he raised the dead (and healed *lepers!*)
before the Romans nailed him—as they nailed all such—
and the neighbors sniffed, "He didn't come to much!"

ANNUNCIATION

She didn't notice at first the air had changed.
She didn't, because she had no expectation
except the moment and what she was doing, absorbed
in it without the slightest reservation.

Things grew brighter, more distinct, themselves,
in a way beyond explaining. This was her home,
yet somehow things grew more homelike. Jars on the shelves
gleamed sharply: tomatoes, peaches, even the crumbs

on the table grew heavy with meaning and a sure repose
as if they were forever. When at last she saw
from the corner of her eye the gold fringe of his robe
she felt no fear, only a glad awe,

the Word already deep inside her as she replied
yes to that she'd chosen all her life.

THE DISCONSOLATE CHIMERA

The crying shadow in the funeral dance,
The loud lament of the disconsolate chimera.
                                    —T. S. Eliot

The disconsolate chimera wandered the waste
where the fasting figure refused to take much notice,
though the dreaming monster offered him a taste
of a perfect loaf of bread. And then—it boasted—

kingdoms and empires of the world, total power
to run everything. But the figure answered no.
And last, at the apex of the trial's hour,
the spiritual strength to bend all things below

to his own will. But the figure looked away,
and the chimera, gathering up its wavering folds
of diaphanous mirage, floated into the sky,
where loud as a thousand banshees its vanishing cry
failed to frighten the figure bowed below,
grieving for all who'd perish on this way.

THE PRODIGAL

She floated before him like a summer cloud,
pink and white through his sweat, and then lay down
squealing, by her sucklings, a teat for each mouth.
The husks caught in his throat. If he'd only known
the pigs would have it better than he, he never . . .
He, ripe offal, stuck in the world's latrine!
—so he told himself over and over and over
and over again. With tears came a keen

ache in his chest. Next day he started home.
He tried to stop his thoughts, lethally busy,
but at night yearned for the slops and warmth of the barn,
the hogs' contented grunting and homely stink. Alone,
he knew he'd failed beyond all hope of mercy.
He didn't even see his father till wrapped in his arms.

PERFECTION

It was the equal of *Amouage* or better,
more expensive than a year's median wage,
and she kept it in a flask the general gave her,
brought all the way from Egypt. "Never age,"

he'd said, "Stay perfect. This will help."
But she was far from perfect and the shame
that'd hardened to a callus over the self
was loosened by the way he spoke her name—

kindly, without contempt. So when that other face
looked deeply into hers, she saw her soul
and what it had become and ran from that place.
Such knowledge burned. Yet she found the bottle

and returned, wiping his feet with her hair,
pouring out herself as her fragrance filled the air.

She had a headache and the kitchen help
were off for the day, when Peter appeared and said
He would be with them for dinner. She herself
could never do things casually. Her head

felt like bursting. She had to send out Mary
to the market, where that dreamer always took
forever to choose the bread, the wine—*hurry*
was a foreign word to her, always sitting in some nook

staring out the window. Then *He* came
with his hungry followers. Martha did her best
to carry out dinner by herself. But she swore
when she saw Mary sitting next to Him on the floor.
To curse might be wicked, but she too deserved rest.
She'd borne the labor and now the company's blame—

Martha... Martha. Peace stunned her as He slowly spoke her name.

LAZARUS

Nothing tasted like a wafer on his tongue.
It wasn't new, he'd tasted it once before—
in the myriad of years before he was,
and *that* took no time at all, the *nothing* before

everything else. As a boy he'd thought about it:
Why was there *anything* at all? The feeling
it led to was pleasant and dark, detached as if
he'd suddenly expanded to fill the ceiling.

And then, of course, the debts, the illness, the quarrels
between his sisters that drove him up the wall—
he'd left all these, thank God! Relief had swirled
through him with the fever until nothing was all.

But now this traveling magician with his meddling work
was drawing him back to his body—cold, stiff, and dark.

He'd been lying there most of his life.
When the angel troubled the water, he couldn't move
fast enough to be first. He had no wife
or brother to carry him: no one that love,

a sense of justice, or pity moved to the task.
So when the wonderworker came, he was resigned
again to seeing someone else cured. He didn't ask,
even when the healer looked him in the eye

and inquired if he wished to be healed—
not a strange question, considering his vocation
of living in hope denied: he was a professional
at it, with status and a certain reputation.

Take up your bed. . . . He obeyed before he thought,
luckily, of all he'd have to learn to live without.

JUDAS

All along I was the only one who seemed to know
what the Man could do if he put his mind to it.
I'd seen him raise the dead, for God's sake, and control
the wind. Rome and her clackering legions would quit

Jerusalem tomorrow if he'd but say the word.
Or, if he wished it, thousands would die for him,
ecstatically falling upon the conqueror
with sticks and stones. So I waited for his least hint

of rebellion. But when he said he might choose
death, and how the Pharisees would see to that,
I couldn't believe him. Surely it was an elaborate ruse.
Surely at any armed threat he'd knock them flat!

He hinted as much to me, and I, conscious of the sin,
supped, betrayed, and kissed, that the battle might begin.

THOMAS

The man was dead. He'd seen. And that was that.
He'd helped them bury him. The heart had stopped.
Later the women started in. Soon all were mad,
jabbering about seeing him, his wounds. They dropped

everything else and huddled to see a ghost
like the gentiles' squeaking wraiths and spooks.
At last he agreed to look but locked the door—no
tricks! Suddenly among them . . . he blinked and looked

twice—*He* was. "Thomas, put your finger here."
Thomas pressed the wounds—the hands, the side—
the flesh all torn pitifully. "My Lord, My God!"
Later He ate the fish and drank the wine

Thomas handed him. Thomas never took his eyes
off him, the living flesh, for which the starved heart cries.

Always there was something at the edge of his eye,
a whiteness, a light trying to break through.
It had led him to Jerusalem a number of times,
this god none could see because too close to view—

the one the poets described, as he had read,
"In him we live and move and have our being."
But he was frustrated, for an inner voice said,
"Spirit is invisible, yet seeing is believing."

Then he met the twelve and all slowly changed:
what Stephen saw was showing in his face
and shone through the witness that he gave
to the council, which sat astonished in that place

and ground their teeth and rushed him, unable to forgive
him for saying that he saw what none can see and live.

Keeping the Law was a bore, the outer part,
that is—nothing for a Pharisee such as he.
But keeping the inner law of the heart—
o perverse self!—to that he lacked the key,
ransacked the whole Sanhedrin. Then one day
an idea seized him: he breathed it in like fire:
something that would consume him totally.
He felt the inner division heal as all conspired

to make him champion of the faith. He offered to go
wherever needed to put them back on the path—
the blasphemers—to hold up the Law against all those
in this semi-pagan cult and bring down the wrath
of Yahweh on them, while sinning not the least mote—
the others stoning them while he held their coats.

PAUL

After Rubens' "The Conversion of St. Paul"

Still breathing threats, he was off to Damascus
with letters to seize the ringleaders of the cult.
At peace with himself, his anger and learning at last
fused, he could now *act*, direct the bolt
to the evil that flickered on the horizon.
He was riding in company, thinking of nothing special
when the lightning struck. He fell blind from his horse.
"Saul," the voice came, "Why . . . ?" And at that, all

his learning tumbled after and his pride. The old division
shot through him: spirit and flesh wrestled, alive.
Gone the peace he found by shutting out that other,
the one who called the God of Moses *Father*
and, worse, claimed that he and the Father were one—
worse still, that Saul the Pharisee had sinned.
Three days passed before he opened his eyes.

THE EPICURE

It was a pleasant life: at night the temple girls,
occasionally, after lunch, the flute-playing boy.
A moderate life: poetry for the heart and prose
to temper the mind, though I found less and less joy
in it, that ineffable something in the humors
of youth. I was middle-aged. Then walking in the agora
I heard one speak of a strange god—surely just rumors—
but there was something in his eye, and I heard Pythagoras'

golden spheres turn for a second: the old joy returned.
Listening to him—scrawny, a head short—I hardly heard
his words for the music that lifted me: someone yearned
through it for me—a face? a light? a darkness? His words
at last trickled in, seeds through a sieve. Since then, this
life's meant cold night watches, fasts, tears . . . bliss.

He was not in his dark cave; he was sun-bathing
on a winter's day, soaking up heat from a rock
when the sun advanced and split in two. In a ring
of light he saw a blazing figure—no great shock
for him, the bronzed feet, eye of fire,
John told his disciples. He was soon reassured
it was his old friend who had spoken in a whisper
when they last ate together. This time he heard

aloud the same glad promise: "If any one opens the door
I will come in to him and eat with him
and he with me"—now John's habit at meals, and more
or less constantly throughout the day: in the dim
evening and morning to eat and be satisfied,
as now in the blaze of noon and when the stars sang to his eyes.

THE SHROUD
(*at Torino*)

> *the wild darkness of the Godhead.*
> —*Jan van Ruysbroeck*

One can read the linen like a battle map,
where the blood advanced, retreated, pooled.
Here the creeks ran with it, there it blistered and dried.
Every detail is patiently recorded
as in monuments we wander through like tourists
vaguely uncomfortable, unwillingly involved.

Still his face rises above this moment
at peace, like a bird carried above the battle,
bearing our days away on wings of light.
We see the love buried in these lips
waiting for the stone to be rolled—heavy clog
of the human heart, ballast of history.

Faint as an old tintype the image
hovers, masking an outrageous light
from the wild darkness of the Godhead,
the ravenous wings of Easter that will stoop
on death scurrying like a spider,
shake the flowers out,
and tumble sparrows in a well of singing—

48

until at last we open and the garden going in
green robes seizes us with laughter
bright and terrible, blowing loose our hearts,
like the Mary shaken from her cloud
to the enormous gaiety of light
and the whole spontaneous flesh
now and forever loved in its first being.

THREE

PEONIES

In June these
globes of white flame
swell, explosions so very
slow, we see in them absolute
fire at the center, stasis
of star's core,

or a fragile
moonglow distilled
ghostly in each alembic.
From their green ambush these
unearthly aliens assault
us with color

for a week
then gradually fade
into another dimension. As
Dante saw the stars in a glass,
a corolla of souls,
each reflecting

the other's light
and charity, so in these
low white spheres we contemplate
mirroring heavens: petals, tongues
stammering silent music from
one root of fire.

THE HUNT

(Welsh form: Cywydd Llosgyrnog)

A locust leaf quivers, is still.
He's gone. I plunge through a well
of light, fall on a root,

leave beetles circling the broken
punk of a dead log. Twigs reckon
my eyes unwakened. Sly, mute

spiders apply theories, webs
that shrivel as I pass. Small dreads
hive in the woods, sting, smart.

A stream—bubbles bead his trail—
wading, images break—to fail
seems a good. Hell swarms with gnats.

Footfalls through long shafts of sun, moon.
Breathing loud, hands my only weapon,
I lunge at last. Self-cheated—

a reek of pelt, a glittering eye,
a chiding of birds. Undone I
turn.
        Mouth wide, he leaps.

It begins with one leaf rubbing against another,
a light, a rift in a cloud, the weight of a feather
spiraling down, a ripple on water—

its shape rising from the dark and fusing
with a sound, a touch, a peculiar scent. Now it begins
to show plumage, the gleam of a pelt, pausing

to stare with an ebony eye. One twitch—it's gone,
fled into that darker wood behind the eyes. Stunned,
you trace its tracks on paper, stumble,

pick yourself up and go down each sly
cheat of a path vanishing in a thicket, lie
still, listening for its breath, a twig breaking

where you think. . . . Avoid sleep, follow all day,
at night listen for its cry under the moon. Finally you may
gather enough to show its presence. Delay

finishing what you have. Take your time. Return home
and frame the cast of its footprint: that is the poem.

1. *The Dream*

At home the year turns slow upon its axis.
July groans from the heat; humid air
drifts slow across a wavering sky,

the sun's red ingot throbbing as it rises.
Trees release faint steaming ghosts
that twist, unravelling from their leaves.

He gives to each a shape where it climbs
above the cherries staggering red
with fruit over the unmown hay:

paladins of summer, seraglios of clouds
with necks like marble towers, while he hears
a tinkling sea-blown music through the haze.

2. *The Journey*

Amulets, anklets, floating mousseline
burn in his eye with sweat. A dry cinch
rots and snaps. The resentful beast

having chewed the cud of anger
destroys the offered fez. Now nothing
hangs in the baked sky but a bird

on wings like ashes in an updraft,
foil for the ego that would find
nothing but itself cloud-hung with ease

among cushions and perfumed servants
where the prayer wheel wanders among mountain bells.

3. *The Desert*

In the acid moonlight, the cold spell,
the drifting dune that gives beneath the foot,
the white waste where the hyena's laugh

comforts, he scans the illegible map:
stars pinpoint his rigorous dreams,
the Lion, the Hunter with his club,

the Twins of ego, alter-ego, the Fish
whose death is a shambles, and the Virgin
whose lamp irradiates the skeleton.

In this hard light, he sees the jackal's bones,
sharp teeth, and snout, the dark declivities
shadowing sight and ravin. Gone, these

fill with the minute trickle of the sand.
Old shadow-face, crouched in the desert sky,
features shrinking with the air

that eats his skin, watches the tides
of desire, projects his shape
against the barren surface of the rock.

4. *The Mountains*

In the far passes, all goods gone,
naked as that hermit of Tibet
whose breath clings to the ice walls of his cave,

saving his shrunken pulse in a moss of thought,
the traveler, having watched his last mule drop,
bells tinkling, down the avalanche,

turn over once and disappear,
despairs of his destination, takes a small
cloud drifting nowhere as his soul,

and at his wit's end makes a lucky guess
at a pass that twists and drops toward terraced slopes,
emerald with new shoots and fireflies
of lanterns marking here and there a hut.

5. *The Outer Kingdom*

Inside the outer kingdom of the Khan
glimmer the inner kingdoms; a golden passport
opens each gate. The inner surround

the ever more interior, elusive
penetralia: a shimmer of kimonos, jade,
lapis, and the solitary bell.

A flute or drum now shapes the grove
where paths broaden. The bridges wax ornate
with teak, ivory, and peacocks screaming

at apes in scarlet jackets. There is no end,
one within the other. He used to dream that
one day the great bronze doors with dragons,

each grasping half a world, would open,
the gong sound, and there at last,
prostrate, he'd slowly lift his head

to follow the golden incense up. . . . Instead,
light of step, he wanders mountain, terrace,
valley, in and out—his camels loose

beyond the flickering palms. He, drunk on air,
the horizon toppling all things to his eye,
follows the elusive flute-note in his heart.

TRAHERNE

The corn was orient and immortal wheat, which never
should be reaped, nor was ever sown. I thought it
had stood from everlasting to everlasting. The dust
and stones of the street were as precious as gold;
the gates were at first the end of the world.
                                        —*Centuries*

1

In God's green camp you sit in a silk tent,
flowers springing under your feet, intent upon
marigolds, goldenrod—sweet ragweed—
Ferdinand forgetful of the fly
which shakes the air with its small news of war.
The ramparts of the camp unwatched, you think:

Let Charles the Martyre go and Cromwell come,
turning his ear to horn inside the coach
while George Fox running beside it shouts for peace—
still at the still point Thy Kingdom comes.

We marvel how an angel like you came—
when precious stones were smoothed for every sling
that flickered at Goliath in the clouds—
to gather ordinary stones from the road
and wash them till they shone in a sluice of light.

2

The smallest grain of wheat would light the ground
like the sun or perhaps the moon gorging
on the summer air—
                              each drop of dew,
a world lying spendthrift in the grass,
and the sky dreaming between wheel-ruts
an image of the soul.
                              In the best sense simple,
each word is a single drop in a still pool,
a leaf turned up by the barest stitch of wind,
accommodating as the edge of a lake and yet
resting at its own level.

          To read your prose we need a kind
of smoked glass. Each sentence flashes like gold
dredged from the sea's grave—the absolutely
real, from which we startle like fish
streaking to hide in a thick net of dreams.

3

Suppose a river, a drop of water, an apple, or a sand.
Suppose the object in the patina of being,
cushioned on the infinitude of God, a light shifting
like a rainbow on the lake's sandy bottom.

Here is the promised rest—a motion and a rest—
the soul, Ezekiel's wheel full of eyes,
wings unfurling candescent Beatrice
while red and white and green dancers shift their ground.

Suppose a curious and fair woman, like this one
tense with the lineaments of fire,
busy about the two infernal refugees
dragged from the pit.
                              The poet turns to his guide,
the film through which everything might be borne—
gone, nothing now but fire beating air.

New Year

The sky is so blue history has vanished.
Each pine stands unentangled in the sun,

knowing the freedom of light, a fringe of snow.
The white forest floor is clean and smooth.

The tracks of chipmunk, mouse, and vole
are tentative, a wandering text to read

with nose or eye, saying what was never said
before this instant—the sun sprung from Eden

like that red fruit before its skin was broken
and knowledge was an unread story, an aroma

on which the soul got drunk. Each footprint's
shadow is new upon the snow, a word

transfixing body and spirit, a light that
never was on sea or mountain, springing

somewhere from the mind's root. Bless now
these graceful figures, a 2, an *O*, an *O*,

a 5, and free us from all false beginnings
accumulated in the past so we can live

this moment as it is, a beginning
with a middle and an end,

that in itself contains all other moments.

In the Solar Room

Sitting in the sun behind the glass doors,
the snow like a brilliant floor of clouds in the garden,

I squint, look aside, knocking on the darkness,
the light pooling at my feet and rising up

past my knees, belly, sternum, to my throat,
pausing, and at last, filling my head

like thick nectar, like a wild electron,
so fast it is in every place at once.

Resting there, feeling the presence grow
intimior, feeling the simplicity, the one—

the eye through which we see each other, the same
eye, as Eckhart said, a steady presence

never not here, never not there. I am ashamed
at what falls under the instant of forgetting,

when the one becomes two, two, the many things,
and I, like fractured light, a thousand shadows.

BORROWDALE, THE LAKE DISTRICT

On a green swell of land the light lies in blisters.
Ravens fall down a bright slant of sky
while mountains go off dreaming to the sea,
each with a lake in tow.

Stone houses shamble in all the corners,
windows unbuttoned and weeds in their hair,
gaping at an angle of sky.

And the sheep—rocks come alive
staring out of ferns woolly with light,
throwing their odd tinny cries against the fells.

Today we picnic under Castle Crag
on the ghyll crawling up from Borrowdale
to stretch out in the sun.

Here is sunlight in a basket.
Here is water white against the teeth,
grass sprung from the most secret ventricle.

All the day lies in this bright circle:
My daughters kicking the water to flame,
the lambs a broken, bleating cloud.

LIGHT YEARS

Light from the earth is traveling in space,
the whole history of the earth expanding into the galaxy,

five, perhaps ten, thousand years of recorded time,
five or ten thousand light-years out there,

aiming beyond the Milky Way, toward intergalactic cold
toward even stranger journeys through other galaxies

that turn in their own spirals, unspooling their histories,
(not to mention the five hundred million possible worlds in ours).

Imagine the photons carrying brief, lost images
of two people gazing at each other for the first time

and thinking it is love, it is forever—a moment
that will endure, whether caught on film or not,

going nakedly into space, into endless travel
lasting as long as time does, though long forgotten here,

but not by those who live still in its light,
the moment's: a green wave arching over the sand.

Raphael's wings are gold, an airy gold that thins
to transparency like sun falling on a wall
and yet deep and wide as sun taking
a field full in the morning or
burning wheat in the eve-
ning. When he flies
away, they are a
streak of salmon or
carmine along the curve of
the sea, and where his feet touch
last, whitecaps rise to rollers and throw
themselves in ecstatic, bright h o s a n n a s
o v e r   and over against the eroding   s h o r e .

A.M.

Yellow flames flutter
about the feeder:
a Pentecost of finches.

MORNING'S AT SEVEN

1. Waking Up

Today the sky is
butter on my bread.
Before I woke, the sun
climbed the white clapboards

inch by inch. I came to,
threw out the night's trash
and tried too hard. But you
had been there all the time
in the rug's green fibers
saturated by sunlight,
holding me up.

I used to slouch down
to breakfast, counting
sixteen lead beads
on a string.

Now the hours are dandelions,
butterchins, peaches—
I hear the stones plop in the garbage
as I open their golden mouths
one by one.

2. Finished

It is finished.
You have done
everything.
I am stunned.

There is nothing
left to do.
The house breathes
a sigh of relief.

All its joists, free
of years of support,
dissolve in the woods
to a rap of distant woodpeckers.

3. A Million Inches of Grass

Getting up today I found
a million inches of grassblade
grown overnight in my back yard.

Something had to be done.
With its usual whirr and thump
my mind pounced on the radio,

the endless static of desire.
I slouched to the bathroom, sick
of the mess of dead skin cells.

At the scratch of my razor, you
woke me to the snowfield of lather,
the red glittering drop on my chin.

4. Dandelions

A galaxy expanding
through green space.
My lawn's a shambles,
clay shows
in pocks and ruts.

My neighbors shave
theirs. I
weak with laughter
among the violets
unleash a thousand roaring suns.

5. Sirius, The Dog Star

Dandelions explode
in the green heart of space.
Supernovae radio
static of a different music.

Between them violets lurk,
ionized purple gases,
nebulae that bend right
off the spectrum.

71

Among them the dog moves,
an unleashed constellation.
Black holes, white holes—
elusive quasars—

he takes them all in
a mind of pure smells,
reading news of the cosmos.
Again his pink tongue

slips out, trembling,
polishes his wet, black nose.

EASY RIDER

Gold fills my fingertips.
My heart keeps
count behind and just

above the garage. Blue,
colloped by the harp-strung
locust, drowns my iris.

My stomach cruises
under the Pole's green ice.
Unknown to mankind

my left foot
passed through Arcturus
yesterday.

Love, love, easy rider,
put me back together but put
the world inside me now—

small lethal puzzle
of scuffed and intricate
beauty heart must hold to.

Half a Second

A movement like a shutter's
and I am outside the dark box—
the ship suddenly outside the bottle.

Instead of empty, everything is full.
There is no absence:
every sail luffs out, every rope sings.

There is no more to be said.
There never was,
but one goes on saying. It is

the hopeless addiction of the tongue
to an ecstasy of particulars:
the snap of young peas, the onion's bite,

the tomato's pulsing alarm
the lupine's lavender finial,
the white cat by the feeder

in a raptus of hummingbirds.
Not only this place, this time,
but all places, all time:

everywhere—nowhere.
It is freedom, it is laughter.
Closing the eyelids and raising them.
That white cloud hanging there forever.

A Song of Praises

for the gray nudge of dawn at the window
for the chill that hangs around the bed and slips
   its cold tongue under the covers
for the cat who walks over my face purring murderously
for the warmth of the hip next to mine and sweet lethargy
for the cranking up of the will until it turns me out of bed
for the robe's caress along arm and neck
for the welcome of hot water, the dissolving of
   the night's stiff mask in the warm washcloth
for the light along the white porcelain sink
for the toothbrush's savory invasion of the tomb of the mouth
   and resurrection of the breath
for the warm lather and the clean scrape of the razor
   and the skin smooth and pink that emerges
for the steam of the shower, the apprehensive shiver and then
   its warm enfolding of the shoulders
   its falling on the head like grace
   its anointing of the whole body
   and the soap's smooth absolution
for the rough nap of the towel and its message to each skin cell
for the hairbrush's pulling and pulling,
   waking the root of each hair
for the reassuring snap of elastic
for the hug of the belt that pulls all together

for the smell of coffee rising up the stairs announcing paradise
for the glass of golden juice in which light is condensed
   and the grapefruit's sweet flesh
for the incense of butter on toast
for the eggs like two peaks over which the sun rises
   and the jam for which the strawberries of summer have
   saved themselves

for the light whose long shaft lifts the kitchen
   into the realms of day
for Mozart elegantly measuring out the gazebos
   of heaven on the radio
and for her face, for whom the kettle sings, the coffee percs,
   and all the yellow birds in the wallpaper spread their wings.

AUBADE

1

Then shall all the trees of the wood sing for joy
   while each leaf thrusts into the universe of air
and the light green haze of April rises like smoke
   sweet in the nostril. Let the mind fill the hemisphere
of day while the sun beats a million white wings.
   Let each yellow and red bud in the dew
blaze forth with a hundred suns while night
   picks up her gauze and vanishes over the hills.
Let the rabbit's eye shine while he drums the turf
   summoning his brethren;
the squirrels spiral down, their tails like clouds,
   to clatter among the woodsy rubble;
and the shrew shriek and hide herself under the root.

2

The cat stretches by the window and cries at the door;
     the dog yawns, then yelps at the rising sun
that will run all day till it drops in the west.
     The mattress creaks as the man rises to fix breakfast,
his back telling him he is—ah!—alive
     while the neighbor's car snorts and gulps air
in an ascending whine.
     Children feel their way through cool porcelain bathrooms,
teenagers dream a world of shimmering electric presences
     and clothes rise from the dresser to glide across the skin,
the belt firmly encircles the waist
     and the tie mounts to prop the chin.

3

Yet, staring back from the bathroom mirror are
     the ghost of the office, the boss's purposeful smile,
fog of the night's dream, the nattering conscience,
     the gluttonous mortgage, the skin in love with gravity,
and the razor's unkind cut—awareness of
     what is done and undone—the thousand engines of destruction
the cerebral cortex draws across its synapses
     toward the fragile sanctum of the present moment.
Let each ghost wither and vanish in sunlight,
     crisp to the nothing it is,
while a joyful procession dances along
     the myriad lightning pathways of the mind.

Tree and house are clear in this moment
    when light is given shape and each thing pauses,
itself—before the frame blurs, the attention fails
    and we fall into one or another distraction:
the horrors and banalities of the news, the half-typed letter,
    the mysteries of long division, the tumbled tower of blocks,
regret's heavy shadow or the usual obsession.
    Lord, in the bright vehicle of this moment,
descend to us and spread your golden tent
    that we might keep sweet breakfast together, your beard dripping
honey as we ascend the dayspring of your eyes
    into an emptiness that is present, solid, and real.

Neti, Neti

Are you the ragged yellow fields?
    No, the grass, broken and happy.
Are you the air, damp and intimate?
    No, the deer's flag, her hoof muffled in the swamp.
Are you the sun patiently peeling the clouds?
    No, the star in the dawn's throat.
Are you the stones bearing me up on their safari?
    No, the acorn's hat, where its thought grows sweet and whole.

    I am all these, and yet none:
Not the red streams flooding the banks of cells.
    nor the river hungry for the ocean
nor the crow's feather that dandles to the ground
    nor the wind trafficking in perfume
nor the little pool holding a syllable of water.

Still, I am where the tongue presses the roof of the mouth,
    in the crease of the closed hand,
in the foot hesitating on the stoop,
      in the eye that draws its shape on the sky
        and lingers, waiting for the face of light.

SELECTED POEMS

FROM *The Waters Under the Earth*

CARRYING THE FATHER

Pater....Ipse subibo umeris, nec me labor iste gravabit.
— *Aeneas to Anchises*

1

From here I carry him upon my back.
He is no longer heavy, though sometimes I
stumble over grief. In fact, he is

thin as the wing on an October fly,
seen through as if not there at all, but in
a certain light suddenly ablaze,

a transparent map of all my life.
He's here, and his voice runs through
my bones and through the roots of my hair.

2

We are at Gettysburg on the observation tower
of Little Round Top. He in his summer khakis
tells how the gray soldiers came on.

83

I am five; the trees are green moving ranks.
Later, in the museum he shows me
the yellowing jawbone of a drummer

and hands me in their green patina
musket balls dug up, a pyramid
still my paperweight. Like him,

these words are more than I can carry,
yet in a draft from the window float
from my desk to the floor.

3

We push open the door to the cabin,
met by a sweet and musty cold, the tick
of mice in the rafters. The electric lantern

shines on the black, shuttered windows,
the furniture sleeping under white sheets.
You crouch: a blue spurt, a flame

crawls up birch bark in the fireplace,
yellow, orange, a hand's width
of warmth reaching out. A stirring, crackling,

and the whole hearth is ablaze and roars,
the log walls leap and shake with light.
Outside, you open the first cream shutter

84

which I unhook from inside. Blue sky
drops in foursquare, the sun blinding,
the thin birch leaves a transparent

green melting in the May light. Now,
all windows open, a warm wind of pine
cedar, and smoke flows through the room.

You hand me the cold icehouse keys and say,
Open it, take the boat out, anchor, oars.
Tonight when the moon goes in, the walleyes
will hit and hit hard, hungry from the winter.

4

Those sweltering days you came home early,
jacket over your shoulder, white sleeves rolled,
we walked to the air-conditioned theater,

through colored shadows entered the same dream.
Or, better yet, while the sun retreated
behind smoke-blue elms, we walked over

to the park where, far off, we heard
faint shouts and smelled the chlorine from the pool.
Down in that damp dressing room my trunks,

still wet from afternoon, coiled cold
around my shivering thighs. The fur on your chest
kept you warm, you said, as we showered

and waded the footbath to the flashing water
not yet streaked with overhead lights, pink
in the fading humid afterglow.

You heaved into the pool, rising like a walrus,
water streaming silver down your red face,
and yelled as you swam to dunk me—

letting me dunk you back, push the weight
of your body under water, light as I was.
You lay there, pretending the dead man's float,

then rose up with a roar and a laugh
while I fled, climbing the ladder
to the high dive, calling for you to watch me

where, reckless, bouncing on the edge
of that heavy board shuddering like a tongue
about to speak its first clumsy word,

I plunged headfirst into the summer air.

5

Mother in her white dress with yellow flowers
crossing the green in Washington during the war,
my sister and I running alongside to keep up—

always at the end of the eight-millimeter film
before the white spots erase the space
and time runs out over and over.

White dress with flowers that I remember,
carrying the summer with her, the sweet smell,
the soft touch, the words, the laughter.

In that white summer evening by the Potomac
she is the whiter center
of the picnic, the soft clink of silver glasses,

while I, running breathless over the lawn
on which I've fallen, stains on both knees,
smell the green mystery. She moves like a cloud

with flowers out of the sky reaching to me,
lifting me, the earth rising up, the grass,
with the shouts of children: *Oley oley ocean free.* . . .

Every Christmas you showed this to us, Father,
together with the scene where you wave goodbye
from the Chevy window, the peak of your cap

cutting a shadow across your eyes. At the white
spots we'd cry, "Stop. Run it backwards."
And you did. Quickly, jerkily,

time and space knit together
until the picture was frozen on the sheet
hanging crooked, a wrinkle running through it,

while we sat there, wanting
somehow to hold the trees, flowers, faces
down to that very day, reaching out

in the darkness for what was always slipping
by, even as we pressed it to us
forever: earth too heavy, too light.

6

It is dark and cold, the high night sky
black as a hat.
Stars like fish swim as you lean

on the rake, now and then stir the coals
of the last few leaves, their heavy ghosts
filling my head, shaking a star or two as they rise.

A small flame leaps: a yellow maple
leaf curls like a fist down to its glowing bones.
In its brief flare your face is

orange, your hatbrim lights from underneath
and your red-checked shirt glows and goes out.
In the dark your shadow beside me says,

"Do you see the Great Bear, the Little Bear?"—
pointing with the handle of your rake, its shadow
arcing across the heavens—

"Those three stars are the belt of Orion, the Hunter.
There's his bow, there his feet where he climbs
up the sky, silently crossing it all winter."

7

In Florida, which you never liked, you fell again,
missing a step on the patio, breaking your hip,
while dizzy with Parkinson's, planting the *impatiens*.

Disgusted with yourself, you lay an hour,
until mother returned; then you calmly gave orders
to the doctor and medics as they carried you out;

over the next four years fell again and again
trying to walk, until it was a joke with you—
how hard your head, how soft the furniture.

After the massive heart attack, they found
no pulse for five minutes, but you came back,
disappointed (you said later) they revived you.

Grown used to your miraculous escapes, we weren't
ready when my sister called and said
you had died quietly, riding in the car

with Mother. The medics worked an hour
while you, no doubt, hovered over them, kibitzing,
floating in the too-white Florida sky,

telling them to leave well enough alone, ready
after years trapped in that wheelchair,
like Orion to take the sky in one long stride.

8

Father, I have just begun to carry you
toward the strange country of the rest of my life
with the household gods and the whole past,

away from the ashes and the smoking walls
across an ocean whose waves rise steep and blue
to the continent of the future, where I shall set you down

flat and weightless, except when you rise like this
from a small gesture, tine of a rake, or ghost
of a burning leaf to your full height and voice

and speak to me even as the light shows through
your flesh, and every scar on your leather jacket
stands out sharp and clear and your voice builds

as you say, *Do not forget the dark
dear past from which all the shapes come, the rich
drift and sleep of leaves over and over,*

*this soil ever crumbling
in which you lay the still invisible garden.*

for Frederick William Siegel and Lucille Chance Siegel

90

THE SURGEON AFTER HOURS

Strange how they visit me at 3 a.m.,
  some accusing, some grateful, some both—
faces tight with pain, flushed and heavy, or
  indifferent, anesthetized. They take shape
like patches of fog in my headlights while I
  thread these dark streets home. They come
beseeching, pleading with me, though I can
  no longer help them, nor tell them not to come,
or rise transcendent with resignation as if they know
  something I don't—I, the technician hired
to postpone the inevitable. They rise up
  like this one, the woman whose heart
stopped under the knife for seven minutes.
  Later, she said she'd died and seen a peculiar light.
I don't recall her words, only her face
  when she tried to say just what it was she saw—
that and the way her hand, birdlike,
  flew over the bedclothes. I wonder,
do our brain cells at the edge
  burst with a final energy? Is the last
illusion more real than life? I don't know:
  hallucination won't explain it, explains
nothing, really. The divisible flesh both is
  and isn't us—that much I feel and more:
we are the whole left when the parts are gone.
  Something surrounds us
we have to lose everything else to find.

FIREWORKS

A few reports at midnight the night before
opened spaces in the sky and in my sleep,
and by the early morning of the Fourth
the bittersweet smell was lurking in the air.
For weeks I'd stared at mauve, green,
and red rice paper packets of firecrackers
covered with mystical Chinese characters,
contraband I'd saved for all that winter—
round cherry bombs, bottle rockets,
whizzbangs, Roman candles, ladyfingers,
shipped in a plain brown cardboard box.

Behind Dick Leckband's house that afternoon
we blew up toy entrenchments, bushes, crabgrass,
whole strings dissolving, drifting down in flakes,
cans rocketing through the air over cannoncrackers,
rattling windows until a cruiser idled by,
its red light flashing like a Roman candle.

At dusk with cousins, aunts, and uncles,
we hurried to the park and the town's display,
spreading blankets in the growing dark,
waiting forever, dizzy with yearning, until
unannounced, except for a fizz of sparks,
a solo rocket cracked open the heavens.

Sighing together in a wave, we watched
pure silver scrawl across the sky, golden rain,
green crowns of light and red Ezekiel's wheels,
purple cataracts, orange asters, yellow fountains—
the whole earth blooming in the heavens
again and again and again while we gazed up
from the dark void at fire spreading out
in a recurring pattern each time different:
the secret work of gravity and light
by which everything came suddenly out of nothing,
fading back into it, rising and falling,
until the end when the American flag
unfurled and blazed brilliantly on its wire
down to a coal, leaving a sweet haze
we walked home through in the double dark
among the crowds murmuring like leaves.
Eyes, ears sated, too tired almost to move,
we stumbled beside our parents who were lost
in talk of ordinary things as if they hadn't
just seen the worlds created and expire.

Drunk on the lingering smoke and its fled music,
hot and sticky, we climbed upstairs
to the sheets glowing in the white summer night
where, scarcely out of our clothes, we fell asleep
to dream in that fecund darkness of the light,
the beginning and end and all things in between.

for Richard Leckband, 1940–2002

93

THE HUNTER

Orion walks again, the night
black and moist with leaves,
chill with the buried smells
rising from wet grass. The earth
tilts once more toward this hunter,
again offering him what

he has not found, though he never
increases nor slackens his pace.
The cartridges in his belt
burnish bright as ever,
the long barrel hanging down
gleams with blueing. He breathes

the cold promise of autumn
which each year lifts his heart
to fields of unseen game
beyond the glittering leaves
and thickets of stars.
Shouldering the moon he climbs

half a hemisphere. Yet
always at the instant he closes
the azimuth of desire,
the world turns and he falls,
fading in the gradual light
that blots him from the sky.

Still, each dusk he returns—
chalk points on a board,
a map, an ancient circuit
imprinted on the skull,
mirroring the shape of the heavens.
His body wrapped in night,

his face shadowed by stars,
he places one foot on the sky,
stalking his quarry forever.

The Very First Dream of Morning

The sun puts in a slow stick
  and touches everything green.
    He hears the mosquito-whine
      of a motor grow louder, then
    a cluck and thump as it stops.
A shadow wavers over him.

He ignores the thin silver line
  flung like a spider's filament
    from a shadowy center again
      and again. The shadow leaves,
    the sun finishes its leap,
and still he hasn't moved

from under the log whose edges
  sway with moss. A turtle
    pokes out its head, pulls it in.
      The surface silvers, blackens.
    A yellow worm of a moon
writhes on the water.

Except for his flowering gills,
  he is motionless, waiting
    until sun and moon darken
      and the lake disappears in a mist—
    when someone, unprepared,
will cry out as if in sleep,

hands fumbling for the reel,
   knowing he has been struck
      (as the pole bends, pulling him down,
         and the boat nearly capsizes)
      by what rises from under the surface
   like the very first dream of morning.

Going On

Once I am sure there's nothing going on
I step inside. . . . —Philip Larkin, *"Church Going"*

Once I am sure that something's going on
I enter, tired of mere ritual,
of liturgy where no work is done,
of punctual repetitions. One can tell
by the face and gestures of the celebrant—
or, better, by the others celebrating
this continually renewed act
of grace (invisible except where a look can't
hide the intimate and present fact).

I go forward, even though mostly summer
is sitting, damp and musty, in the pews,
to where a few in the mid-week evening glimmer
raise hands standing, while others move
to kneel where the priest lays hands on them,
often saying words better than he knows
to say. There I stay until the end
of the service—once more hear the strong love
commending me to eat that I might live.

And so I do. This church's architecture
is nothing special. There are few monuments
or memorials present here.
Only the window in the sanctuary has yet
embraced stained glass. The walls are bare.
What happens here is rarely to be discovered
in anything but the people—well- or ill-favored,
oppressed by poverty, by wealth, by having spent
themselves to no purpose. None is good,

in our first understanding of that word. All come
with a sense, dim or clear, that what they amount to fails,
the intelligence that tirelessly adds up the sum
of things in a clear system, sparks, falters,
shorts out—leaving us to press the mystery
against the roof of the mouth, to hug the ghost
once fused with flesh and still enfleshed in us,
until our spirit answers *Abba* and we know
by living contact what we can't deduce.

It is in the faces, and these come and go
like the spirit, which wanders where it will.
Even Canterbury's merely a heap of stones
until the spirit enters there and wells
in living voices, and thirty bishops dance
gravely to a voice beyond the chancel's.
Let no elegy hang here like the ghost of incense.
Rather, let walls tumble, altars grow wild—new
ones will be raised up in three days (or less)
of the sort the living spirit passes through.

*Note: The dance of bishops occurred spontaneously
in Canterbury Cathedral a few years ago.*

AFTER VIEWING THE BUST OF NEFERTITI

for Ann

> *Dal primo giorno ch'i' vidi il suo viso*
> *in questa vita, infino a questa vista,*
> *non m'è il seguire al mio cantar preciso.*
>
> — *Dante*

Dear, you may not contest it: you
are beautiful as Nefertiti. True,
her nose, her smile, her swept-back eye
which gaze out at eternity
may not be *quite* as perfect, yet,
pity the helpless sculptor set
to render the impossible!
Likewise, if some reader will
reject my awkward verses' thesis
that you rival Akhnaten's princess,
the fault is mine: you are above
the clumsy measure of my love,
or anyone's. No matter how
skillful the hand that traced your brow,
the line would falter. You, my Love,
without her crown or make-up done
to please a pharaoh's humor, still
are beautiful—at the breakfast table,
delightfully disheveled, able
to vanquish all those others doomed
to be perpetually well-groomed.

100

Whether stooping among your flowers
or in more meditative hours,
the cup moving toward you at the rail,
a likeness of you will only fail
to reveal the *je ne sais quoi* that
grows where flesh leaves off—a light
Raphael released from paper, yet
beyond words startled into flight
by this poor pen—the shadow of one
who thought of you before the sun
was kindled, yet precisely here
and for this moment made you the dear
image of that beauty and grace
who loves us with a human face.

Spring Peepers

Listen, as the cries of spring peepers
like ghostly minnows
swim this way, now that, through
the naked woods,
moonfish seeking their home.

The moon's pale laquearia
flash upon the water,
the peeping is more insistent,
a whistling tide.
The deep croak of the elders underpins it—

the lime green, the light brown,
the dark green bull with his red earrings
hidden in the murk.
This amphibious symphony
shakes the roots of trees and the nervous buds,

lifts them toward the hologram of stars.
Shrill notes rinse the hollow rocks,
cleanse the hidden waters
running where streams
suck them to the deep ocean,

The frog hibernates in the heart,
come spring, awakes,
leaps and leaps,
sending his laser cries into the blood.
We sleep with short galvanic twitches,

dream of falling,
wake to moonlight burning along the floor,
spilling over the windowsill,
and follow barefoot into the grasses,
our pajama legs soaking up the dew,

down to the edge of the lawn
where the rain makes the ground unsteady,
the thirsty ear drinking in
these arias, duets, choruses,
these nightlong operas, oratorios

of swamp and woods,
these litanies of ascending summer,
from the intimate, singing auricles of the heart.

TURTLES

They have thought upon this log
since before Socrates
climbed into the light,
or Plato

settled for silence,
or Aristotle
brought out his bottles
and labels.

Each crawls up on a deadhead
with the other philosophers.
Dull as old coins, old helmets,
they do not speak,

but there are subtle
inflections of the throat,
and eyes, half-lidded,
which stare at a question,

and a mouth that holds onto
a conclusion.
Each day adds to their library
a reflection of twigs,

a silver razzle of minnows,
or a new shade of green.
Though their council is old,
no one has spoken.

Sunlight like moss
heavy on his tongue,
their chairman is still
clearing his throat.

ALLIGATOR

I gather like an idea
on the calm waters.
My nostrils, eyes, surface

without your noticing. Then,
like the first dry land from primeval waters,
in an uncertain mist,

suddenly I am there, my low profile steady,
where you saw only a log, a bit of deadwood.
I am a museum

of the Triassic, a special effect
come into sharp focus, my smile
long and obscene.

Each square of my hide is mapped out
like a city block,
my tail curving toward infinity.

When I open my mouth my teeth appear to be
some huge joke,
a Carlsbad of destruction,

My jowls are heavy with secrets and my belly
drags like a rich purse.
Hungry, I explode from the sawgrass,

take the rabbit or stray spaniel into my exchequer
before you notice, so quickly I slide under.
Running deep, I am off

for other sea lanes, other tonnage, but first
settle in the depths a while, full,
the idea of myself

spreading through me from teeth to tail,
basking heliotropic,
the sun a tiny point within my brain.

But night comes
and my tail moves, oar and rudder.
A dreadnaught sliding from its berth,

I sail in the dark on an unknown mission,
Nelson toward the Nile,
or Yamamoto toward Pearl.

I steam with no running lights toward another
inexplicable surprise.
My decks are cleared for battle while I move

silently. When I open my mouth
my teeth are rows of cannon, port and starboard.
I carry myself like a big stick,

a log so ancient, watersoaked,
it floats below the surface sodden, stiff,
but writhe like a single sinew, a green bolt

of lightning at a simple touch,
going after the pig, the chicken, the crane.
I am a mobile mouth, I live to swallow,

teeth within teeth within teeth.
I keep the waterways open for commerce.
I have the smile of a cruiser,

the charm of *The Natchez Belle*
smoking and sparking into Memphis, beating
the water to a waltz,

silks and shivering torchlights in my eyes.

MUSSEL

I am
tasting the ocean
one mouthful at a time.

It is a slow rumination,
a reading of incunabula
in my cloister,

in this cell where light
fills me totally like an eye,
then washes away.

It is a sifting, sifting
as the animalcules make
a tiny crystalline circus.

I collect essences
while the Atlantic waits
for the Sea of Japan—

it is only a matter of time.
Meanwhile each raising of my shell
stirs all the waters of the earth.

The slow tides call me home
but I stay and savor
these identical moments

that pass and pass
in a still monochrome.
I have a single foot

and can make short journeys
out of this box,
its lid gleaming above me.

The myriads rush over me,
the small translucent beings
with their armature

and transparent tubes
swept by the slightest current,
heaped up in cities,

evaporated on a rock.
I close like night upon them.
They become my slow thought

rising toward that light which floats
over me in the dark,
spreading itself on the waters.

Soon I will be ready to leave.
When the light swallows me
part of me will hesitate,

hang back at the hinge,
a little bit of flesh revealing
the radiance of my absence.

SILVERFISH

It lives in the damps of rejection,
  in the dark drain, feeding upon the effluvia
  of what we are, of what we've already been.

Everything comes down to this: we are its living—
  the fallen hair, the fingernail, the grease from a pore,
  used toothpaste, a detritus of whiskers and dead skin.

All this comes down and worries it into life,
  its body soft as lymph, a living expectoration,
  a glorified rheum. In the silent morning

when we least expect it, it is there
  on the gleaming white porcelain: the silver scales,
  the many feelers *busy busy*, so fast, it is

unnerving, causing a certain panic in us,
  a galvanic revulsion *(Will it reach us*
  before we reach it?), its body

translucent, indefinable, an electric jelly
  moving with beautiful sweeps of the feet
    like a sinuous trireme, delicate and indecent,

sexual and cleopatric. It moves for a moment
  in the light, while its silver flashes and slides,
  and part of us notices an elusive beauty,

an ingenious grace, in what has been cast off.
   As if tears and the invisibly falling dandruff,
     skin cells and eyelashes

returned with an alien and silken intelligence,
   as if chaos were always disintegrating into order,
     elastic and surprising,

as if every cell had a second chance
   to link and glitter and climb toward the light,
     feeling everything as if for the first time—

pausing stunned, stupefied with light.
   Before we, frightened by such possibilities,
     with a large wad of tissue come down on it,

and crush it until it is nothing
   but dampness and legs, an oily smear
     writing a broken Sanskrit on the paper,

a message we choose not to read
   before committing it to the water
     swirling blankly at our touch,

hoping that will take care of it,
   trying not to think of it—the dark
     from which it will rise again.

EVENING WOLVES

. . . fiercer than evening wolves.   Habakkuk. 1:8

Round and round they go on about nothing,
on the platinum compact disk of the moon,
the wolves. Their howls revolve about
the nothing that's eaten your life to its skin
even as it eats the moon to a thin rind.
Each revolution of the sound has a silvery
quaver, a light dip and resolution,
a tremolo, like recordings from the Twenties
of voices sheer and faded as old silk.

Listen, the siren starts up again and circles
in its long ascent and decline about the rim,
its aria of desire and desolation,
a litany of memory and loss
and regret settled into like this broken chair
on a winter evening while the last light falls
unravelled by two flies at the window.
Cooling, they creep and stumble on the sill.

The wolves leave despair like a silver needle singing
in the blood, a fear of the blankness of snow,
of the hot slaver of hunger at your throat,
and the red eyes weaving a knot around you
while the fire gutters and you hear no answer
but a murderous vibration among the trees.

113

Worse still would be the absence of this fear,
locked in this cabin with yourself and the moon,
worse for the head lifted in ululation
to make no sound at all but a dry static,
the O of the empty mouth yawning, the vacant
syllable of the moon fading to a white silence—
no dark accusatory, no gathering of angels,
no judgment of teeth like a necklace of knives,
no unyielding jaws locked to your throat.
The last pain is the absence of all pain.

Just two winter flies, a jot and a tittle,
as the muffled clock beats against the silence
in the empty room, a jot and a tittle
against the solid glass
through which you might make a run for the river,
risking the swift analysis of the teeth
cleaving sinew from joint.

Better to be driven by the pack
through the trees toward the overwhelming sound of
                                                   water
and, desperate, pitch yourself beyond yourself
over the cliff into the cataract,
into the thrash and thunder of Niagara—
risk drowning and a quick oblivion that at last
you might rise again, broken and absolved.

RAT

Peering warily over his moustaches,
with a dozen children to feed,
he pauses where he's pulled himself from the rainpipe
his stare steady but not rude.
It says, his frank beast-like gaze,
that your house is likewise his,
that *mine* and *yours* are an elaborate game you play
as soon as you lay down a threshold.
In a twitch he's gone under the bush and you worry
about foundation holes you forgot to plug.

He is not inconsiderate or impolite.
He simply goes with the grace he has been given
and replicates his kind.
There, and there, they move like night,
faster than moths or oxidation.
At midnight you hear him rattle broken glass
in the dark rafters over your head
while the cat crouches, waiting.

He is neither obtrusive nor violent, this intruder,
and you may forget you've ever met him.
But one day when you've forgotten even more,
he'll gingerly carry away
what no longer troubles your memory:
even those little matters of dress
he excavates for, after a seemly time.
His tooth will not wake you, monotonous, insistent
as a clock for which you have no use.

You will be alone when he carries off bits of your shoe
or bow-tie, watchband or silk pocket,
and, solemnly, I swear you'll not protest
when he carries off the ankle-bone
from which the burden of responsibility has been lifted,
until everything you have is his.

Look on him kindly, for he
at last will carry you to a freedom beyond yourself,
out of the box you have built all your life,
to a sweet disorder in the dust.
There you may rise, sift, and riffle,
dissipate in the wind,
until you are part of everything
you didn't pay attention to while alive.

He will help you find what you talked about
and thought you cherished
until the sun shines through all your spaces
and you bless the water with your absence
and the air is your plain thought—
until all *mine* is *yours*, and *yours* is *mine*
and the words nothing.
                              Meanwhile
look on him kindly,
this ambassador from the Other—
adversary, beneficiary, brother.

A Colt, the Foal of an Ass

Contemplating the dust he stands
in the direct unbearable noon, tethered
to the dead thorn. His long ears hang
down, twitch and revolve as the gang of flies
brassily land and bite and ascend
in a constant small black cloud. His hide
at each bite quivers and smooths out
like this earthquake-tormented land,
while his tail, with its bathrobe tassel, larrups
and swats too late.
                    His eyes, half-lidded
in the bleaching light, are fixed and still,
his plain, dull face perpendicular as a post,
his forelock hanging over it.
                              He does not
turn toward the stranger who stands talking
with the two at the door. Only his muzzle,
soft as silk and still faintly pink,
twitches as his nostrils catch the foreign scent,
widen, and lift his lip for half a second.
                                          Then
lazily he turns to look, eyes glazed, indifferent,
tugs at the harsh rope once, desists,
patient with donkey patience, already learning
the rough discipline that pulled him from the grass
and his mother's side.
                       Now, without warning,
as if he feels a tremor underfoot,
some inaudible alarm from the world's core,

117

he bares his teeth and breaks the air with a sound
like a stone wrenched and crying from its center,
harsh and grating as a rusty hinge
on which the whole earth hangs.

                              Later
there is a moment with a crowd roaring
in surges long and hoarse as breakers crashing,
cool, green branches to tread over the hot stones,
and flowers which offer a brief fragrance underhoof—
one moment of all those in the years that are to come
of fetching and hauling for masters bad and good,
when he does not mind what he is carrying,
when a sense of joy returns, the early smell
of grass while he first stood, unsteady, in the field
with a beast's dim sense of liberty.

Still, he cannot guess what he is carrying
and will not remember this moment in all the years
until he is worn out, lame,
until the hammer is brought down on his unsuspecting head,
his hooves melted to glue, his hide thrown to the crows—
when he shall return to this now, this always,
he continues to live in,
this moment of bearing the man,
a weight that is light and easy,
celebrated in a rough, ecstatic chorus,
toward his own fatal burden heavier than the world.

SLUG

White, moist, orange,
I crawl up the cabbage leaf exposed,
too much like your most intimate parts
to be lovely, to be loved. I weep to the world,
my trail a long tear, defenseless
from its beaks and claws
except for my bitter aftertaste.
He who touches me shares my sorrow
and shudders to the innermost—my pale horns
reaching helpless into the future.
In plastic cups filled with beer
ringed like fortresses around your garden,
your lie of plenty,
we drown by the hundreds,
curled rigid in those amber depths,
so many parentheses surrounding nothing.
You do not understand nothing:
the nakedness to the sky,
the lack of one protective shelter,
the constant journey.
Millions of us wither in the margins
while food rots close by.
Nothing is a light that surrounds us
like the breath of God.

DADDY LONG LEGS

I am a circle. My perimeter moves
in any direction—up, down
sideways, forward. My center
is the center everywhere, for I gather
the world around me where I happen to be.
It is alarming how quickly I climb
your khaki pantleg, then scurry over
the grass you brush me to, climb up a tree
though I seem to have no head for direction,
hurrying and standing still at the same time.
One of me is as good as a thousand, for I
meet myself coming back in passages through time,
matter and anti-matter,
monads and mirrors.
Though I move I am still here
and here and here and here,
my scurrying legs
the mere static of time
in the brilliance of being.

I appear to have no eyes, no ears,
no mouth. I am a single thought
surrounding itself, a singular idea,
an eye staring at the inside of the universe,
a pinpoint of light which holds within itself
the history of the Big Bang
and the revolving archangels of the Deity,
the Pleistocene and Waterloo
and the Grammy awards,
a singularity indeed
from which all flows and circles on itself.

I am brown
as a bun and a cushion button,
my legs thin as hairs.
Where I am, I hold all down
for a moment, then move on
invisible in the grass until
I am again crawling up your arm
as if desperate with a message,
as if to climb the air were no great feat
on invisible threads of light
to give some intelligence of earth to the sun.

A small Martian robot,
a space module, a moving camera,
a heat-measuring spectroscope
gathering the information of surfaces,
computing it and sending it back
as I touch everything lightly,
a measuring up
and radioing of it to a transcendent network—
my legs like the hair of Einstein
or the mad scientist's
or the movies where brains with beaks take over
and siphon everyone up until matter shrivels
and everything is just an empty sleeve
and earth spins away as a colossal thought
into the abyss of thought around it
and there is a vague hosannahing of antennae
and a chorus of small green blips
but gigantic thunders of imagination
and a pure gold dawn when matter reappears.

I am the careless aunt whose hair strays
over a face pregnant with black-eyed susans
and fresh currant-berries,
with babies and poems that flew away in the garden
and a smile that dreams another world into being.
I am what didn't get tucked up when you were a child
and made a wonderful mess in the mud
under the cooking sun, the grass
bleeding into your elbows and knees
and the mud on your chin, the small pebbles
lined up and glittering in a row, your own sweet breath
as you moved things and saw them in a riot of newness.

I am a hot-cross bun on legs,
there for the eating, whose bones contain magic
like peyote
to alter the world. If you bite my center
you will never again be content with peripheries
or the long wastage of halls and the dim shores
of existence on the margin, but catch
the single reedy scratch of the sparrow
straight through your heart—
nor be tired from the hours of waiting and
the gray inconsequentials,
the violet of unfulfilled yearning,
and the fizz of desire,
the sad antics of the calculated moment
and the paper parapets of weeks and months,
but drop into the center
revolving slowly
pulling the world by you like a sea—
a strong swimmer
reaching out and pulling all things past,
lightly touching all surfaces,
taking everything and leaving it as it is,
rich with a word you cannot own.

SNAIL

In the dark backward and abysm of time
I make my home,
    lying here at its mouth
        taking a little sun or reaching
into the slick grass,

    carrying the stone house of the past
with me, its heavy whorls and convolutions.
    I am shy if a stranger comes
        or night or danger
and reach back in, trying to hear

    words from the holy cave of my birth,
    what the shadows said on the flickering wall
    in the light that teased me forward.
        I listen to my own shell
to the ocean of becoming

    to the flock of moons that led us to pasture
    to the stars that foamed on the shore
        tide after tide
            drawing us up
the long climb on sensitive foot

    over hard shingle
    and the myriad shards of the others,
        the white cliffs of bone.
            Inside this smooth-lipped sarcophagus
that has ridden the centuries

I read glyphs on the walls
like the fossils of ferns
that have said something over and over
for a century of millions of years—
the curious bones of the mastodon

and ultrasaurus
that heaved up the sky
then lay down in a puzzle,
the trilobites that carried on wars
flashing coded messages

from under dark helmets
to die in a huddle
under the cliff.
I listen to each century,
its myriad events

that have gone unrecorded,
its dark hesitancies and reticences,
all those moments which crowded past
before they could be contemplated,
the questions answered and unanswered,

the cries in the night.
Here in my coiled horn
I crawl back into the rock
that leaked life in the beginning.
It is my oracle

through which the future speaks clearly
of what has gone before,
  my conch, my ramshorn,
    before which the walls shake and crumble
revealing the corpses in their mortar:

  the uncomplicated green air
  entering the lungs of a vireo
   about to be shot by Audubon,
    or the terrible invisible bacilli
breeding in the blankets of Lord Amherst,

  or the one who lived
  looking from the second storey window
  and recorded it on seraphs of paper.
    (*Seraph/ saraph,* angel/serpent
turning together in the double helix).

  My shell coils one way to life
  and I coil the other way back into it—
   matter and antimatter in a Feynman diagram,
    past and future the points of two cones
whirling into each other,

  weaving consciousness, the brilliant
  funklein of the present moment,
   where all is possible, all is known,
    burning nucleus, homunculus,
the utter penetralium of desire—

this cliff that totters above me,
this library I drag with me,
as I sign my path with tears
silver from my weeping foot,
this exclamation slurred on the rock,

this short word that dissolves
into the path of morning.

The returning honeybee performs a dance to reveal to the others the exact location of the source it has discovered. In the dark hive, the other bees interpret the dance by the air-currents from its wings. —nature film

> *Now imagine what would happen if he went down again to take his former seat in the Cave.*
> *—Socrates*

Having   found   the   gold   treasure

of Atahualpa, the place of gold-dust one

can wade in up to the thighs, I do my dance,

my   wings   and   legs   showing   precisely   its

direction—t h e candle-tree's,   the   o n e

whose gold cups spill over with heaven,

whose   gates of ivory   blush

purple, and whose every   entrance is

an opening to a confessional   where the soul

murmurs and grows drowsy with absolution,

whose royal touch covers it with gold,

there, in the flower's secret part.

The others swarm around me in a fever.

The sceptics urge their questions. There is an edge

of impatience, of anger even, as the zealots

ask   me   to   try   again   and   yet   again

to show precisely that point on the horizon

where   E l   D o r a d o   lies

beyond the bell of our ordinary sky,

the fields and orchards we labor in—to show

exactly where this tree is that is different,

whose blooms are storied lamps breathing,

like Ali Baba's, the seven perfumes

of Babylon—are throats that open

like the fabulous gold lake

of Montezuma, or the gates of pearl.

I am exhausted, and still I repeat the pattern

for those anxious to take off unerringly

to the source, eager to drone back,

bellies heavy with plunder

(so they imagine), freighted with 24-karat

until the cellars spill over, lucent with honey,

a   sea   of   gold   hoarded   away   in   wax.

At   such   times   I   wonder: Could   I   live   this

dream   for   one   eternal   afternoon

w h i l e   l i g h t   s h o n e

blazing   in   the   sky   before   me

and   feel myself   melt   into   it   one   moment

to   which   there   was   no   before   or   after

b u t   o n l y   a n   I S   o f   w i n g s —

and   still   come   back to   this   dark cave

to   fan   its   meaning   on   the   wall

where the others feel nothing

but the current of air from my wings

and   understand   my   directions   only

by blind   intuition — come   back,   wings

frayed,   legs   feeble, to perform

this small dance over and over?

FROM *In A Pig's Eye*

Ego

has thrust his nose under every board,
smelt out every wild carrot and white grub,
stucco'd the dirt with his tracks from side
to side, rubbed smooth the corner
posts, left his pink, red-bristled hide
on every barb of five strands of wire;

chewed the bark from the one scrub pine
that pitches a ghost of shade at noon,
bangs incessantly the metal trough-lid
at off-hours, chuffs down the white meal,
raising a cloud around his ears, and cleans
each cob with the nicety of a Pharisee,

tooth for tooth, squeezing contentedly
his small bagpipe voice as he mashes
corn with a slobbery leer and leaves
turds like cannonballs across a battlefield.
Meanwhile his little pink eye is
periscoped on the main chance—

the gate ajar, the slipped board,
the stray ducky that flusters through the wire—
saliva hanging from his mouth like a crown jewel.
His jowls shake with mirth under the smile
that made a killing on the market, won the fifth caucus,
took the city against all odds.

No wonder we shake at the thought of his getting out
of his square patch, electrify the wire
(At night we hear him thump his dreams
on the corrugated tin hut and shudder,
the single naked bulb in there burning
through our sleep like his eye!),

take special dietary precautions against
his perpetual rut, except that March day
we drag the yearling sow to him
through mud up to his hocks. From that handseling
comes the fat litter—the white one for the Fair,
the spotted black to be slaughtered in November.

We don't show him to the neighbors, though in June,
framed by clover and bees stringing out the sun, he is
quite grand, an enormous blimp supporting
intelligent waggish ears, regally lidded eyes and
a pink glistening snout
ready to shove up the privates of the world.

SOW'S EAR

Here comes a lusty Wooer,
My a Dildin my a Daldin,
Here comes a lusty Wooer,
Lilly bright and shine, A.

Fifty sows dozing in the hard-packed yard,
fifty sows, all sizes, from purple majesty
to pink ninny,
fifty, sluttish, given to untidy houses,
the open robe of morning, flea in the air,
snorting, swilling the hay-strewn water,
some indifferent as the Sierra Madre
steaming over deserts, features lost
in foothills and ridges of fat;
others petulant, bristling,
practicing the small clean bite.

The lean young boar, thick-necked
walks a plank from the truckbed,
razor-backed, tufted, tusks rounded to ball-bearings,
lord of the mountains, the hills of flesh,
the little valleys spread before him.

He is small, but the muscles of his neck
can break a hound, or a man's leg.

First one, sullen, whitish-purple in the heat,
stands off, pegs the dirt—mean hussy—
grunts, *Come show me, Bastard!*
Grunts, and grunts again.

Though he doesn't turn toward her, he sees her.
Still, he waits for her waddling run,
her little yellow teeth
bared for the swipe at his haunch,
swivels and knocks her off balance—
blood pudding, sack of fat!
Terror curdling from her throat, she
telegraphs herself to a far corner,
peg peg peg peg peg.

The second, caught off-guard,
lies where she falls, croaking.
But the third,
mother of clouds and mountains,
400 pounds of mauve-and-pink repose,
feels their cries stoke a fire in her bowels,
a vein of lava creep from marble hams,
through vesuvial lungs,
to the flexing crab of her brain.
Uncertainly, on one leg, then two,
she jacks herself from the primal pool
where gnats nidder and dance.
Mud swings crusted on her teats,
falls in patches from her belly:

What are these that tickled the brain?
Love's tiny cries? The yammering mouths?
Squeals that hang like sausages?
No, not those tender attentions.

Dimly, she remembers something
unlocked from her, a tremor, a quake
an eruption,
when once she opened and
free of her hulk
the delicate she of a dream
danced like rain on a corrugated roof,
pooled in cool wallows,
sprouted under tender thistle,
rolled in goldenrod and clover,
frisked with cat and suckling.

Turning toward him like a locomotive
on its turntable, the steam
of her memories creasing all her jowls
to one truculent smile, she charges:

Oh to be the blue fly, the bee, golden,
jigging above the ticklish purple!
                    BANG
Aye, this is the rub,
the tickle of love! she snorts, enamored.
                    BANG
O honey bee! Sweetling,
hungry for my attentions!
Again she turns where the boar, dizzy
and sore in the neck, stands baffled.
Having assaulted with his head the Himalayas,
having not gotten over the foothills,
he staggers in disbelief
as Everest trundles toward him.

This is the one! Husband! she croons,
full and resonant as a bullfrog,
Sweet chop, my porker, my honey cob!

O what a squall of pipers,
what a regiment of bloodcurdling love,
dooms over the highlands of her corpus
resounding from glen and hillside
as she advances on him in a corner,
stale and snuffed as Macbeth,
head slung low, as all the world marches on him,
to meet the fate, perilous, magnificent,
of fathering five hundred friskers.

A Lady Who Lov'd a Swine

I'll build thee a silver stye,
  Honey, quoth she,
And in it thou shall lye:
  Hoogh, quoth he.

It was those little teeth she loved most
showing at breakfast, the road-mapped
eyes over the shaking O of coffee,
the snuffling and snorting behind the paper,

as if his anger built a factory
behind a paper scaffold, a plant
to electrify her kitchen, made a place
of scorched toast, a Red Sea of counters

drained flat when he left. The ticking
fly-leg in the clock stamped each second.
She'd sit in the elastic mouth
of the armchair, rubbing a purple bruise

he'd given her last night—corsage
aching with color, drunkard's lovebite—
while the air waltzed with dust
and pain roosted in her nest of hair.

The brisk *chnnk* of mail in the box
would send her to the door, opening which
she'd let in the sun in its pert
gossipy way to enquire,

139

How could she stand living with the brute?
Didn't her face need re-upholstering?
She hugged the insult back to bed
like a hotwater bottle.

In the March afternoon she'd try to dig
up bird cries buried in the yard,
something muffled the sun might coax loose,
all the while listening for his shadow

and booming demand for a drink, his beery cheek
sanding her neck as he squashed her to him
tilting toward the icebox and boozy dreams
of swilling all night with the squealing girls.

And she would droop down willingly and listen to the ice
ring music, ring money, under a porcine stare
puerile and crafty—*Dearest, dearest piggy*
of her heart, rooting hot, stamping at the rails,
rummaging the husks of her endless love!

HOG HEAVEN

In some dim sense he sees
it is already here,
the field of delicate corn, the glittering
wallow where each rolls free
of the hill of flesh, of the jawless appetite
that inhales a world of garbage and shrieks *More*
(as if the skin didn't have a decent limit)—
that tries to thrust himself upon himself
until all flesh balloons to one vast Pig
on which he is the smile, satisfied.

Dozing on the warm cement he dreams
that the sun, puzzled, pauses in the heavens,
that *First one at the trough for swill*
and *Furthest from the draft at night*
are not enough,
that the sun-warmed fly, who now forgets to bite,
buzzes another tongue, and the lifting wind
sneaks glittering through the goldenrod
to whisper something else into his ear
before the whistle blows, *It's time for slops.*

Like straw such dreams trouble the water's surface—
the pig's persistent business of stuffing, rutting
and grunting to his fellows his narrow will—
until the box pulls up and the ham-faced farmer
with hands like shovels and two sly-footed dogs,
directs him into terror's empty room
over an engine mumbling and shaking like a fly.
Too late—he cannot think for the squealing mob,
hunger, cold, and dust thick in his snout.

But after three days without water,
sensing the golden sacrifice of bacon,
the roast's crackling holocaust,
he rises, hilarious as helium
and, winged above the anonymous pen,
a winter gaiety glazing his eye,
a seraphic humor slimming his jowl,
foresees and forgives all:
the rotating jaws, the dreamless fat and muscle,
the blank pink hands which lift the plate for more.

BULL

Flies crawling the map of his ear
    do not bother him.
His eye has the long look of history.
    When he blinks
the tizzy settles somewhere else.

On cold mornings he snorts twin
    blue mushrooms, his hide
bearing a starwork of frost
    as if he sprung whole from the sleep
of Babylonian astronomers.

His hoof divides the dust.
    It is precisely out of this scrape
came his appetite for geometry—
    to eat the earth piece by piece.
Then wonder put a hook in his nose

and he lay among milk-white cows
    who sang upon harps of sunlight
swaying in the grasses
    until his heart ran with pity,
gored by a purple wound.

Now with a brass ring for his law
    he stands in a lake of shade
watching us, inconstant white things
    among goldenrod, purple thistle,
alert for the bloody insult—still,

only half a mind to malice,
    dreaming among his blue flowers:
ready to kick the world to static,
    if need be, if need be, but listening,
as the earth builds and the pollen blows,
    to the small crazy song of the bee.

They are foam collecting
     on the shore of the field.
Backs yellow with dust
     they lean against the gate,
now one, now another lifting a voice
     vibrating and torn as the Irish.

They are richly dressed, each wigged
     like a British justice. Yet
they move together like slaves
     bent under Pharaoh,
to be folded into the dark
     eating every green thing
and complaining at the dust of their daily bread.

If March shows the icy
     back of his robe,
they will go no further.
     Eyes thick with rheum
they feel death's finger shake the ground:
     Thousands in one night
rot where they fall like patches of late snow.

Still the old ram carries his head
     like the treasure of Persia,
uttering a melodious question,
     knowing he will be answered
when the sun comes striding
     from the oratorio of the hills
touching his fleece with gold.

145

MUSKIE

Eyes hoarding dull gold he lurks
at the bottom
holding the lake steady
in water the color of bock beer.
He has aged for decades—
in season, out of season.

Above him motors unzip the sky all day
and zip it up again
as he lies under layers of water
turning the drowsy
silk of his fins, watching shapes
panic across his ceiling.

Light fades. The wind drops.
Shapes grow clearer
on the surface, except for a wavering
ghost of birches, the quick cipher
of waterbugs. A yellow lamp
gleams and dissolves.

Then, from under the dark
fallen tree he shoots
on a straight tack, seizing
the sputtering plug, diving
against the light,
shaking the first stars from his tail.

Hauled-in, black and silver,
blood mapping his throat,
chewing the air of a pitiless altitude,
he beats a tattoo
on the aluminum hull, listening
to the deep waters
grow still
more silver in a moon that climbs
finless, among the stars.

She lost him to the dull light
fanning the pier where the submarine
slept on lean haunches. In months to come
the land heaved to the slow
tide of battle, news that
washed across the front pages.

Censored, his letters brought
accounts of boredom, ice cream,
hints of Bombay, Madagascar.
She stuck pins in a map, following
imaginary voyages until some fact
unstuck them all,
teasing her again across the endless
harp of longitudes.

At night his underwater shadow
slid through her dreams
into seas jewelled with disaster.
Pillows nuzzling her breast,
in thunder and lightning she felt
a mortal tremor of ships;
her windows sang like angels
to white ghosts of war.

Bearded, sea-changed,
he returned,
lifting her like the globe
lovingly this way and that,
his duffel spilling
her letters and an ocean's
weight of tears.

Still, the undersea shadow
cruised her dream, its eye
a work of winking light and pearls.
The faint hum and turbulence
of steel shapes passed,
fading to a gull's derisive cry
where waves scribbled
and erased a shore.
Then stiff with sleep he'd rise
and take her in arms
blue from the ocean.

The dreams passed.
At last, only her letters recalled
secretly to themselves
her underwater fear,
the long tapestry of nights
by which she shuttled him home
crabwise from the sea,
beggar with a star pinned to his shoulder.

Now They Stand Still

Horses grazing by the river
stamp and raise their heads,
proud in the mirror of each other's gaze,
forelocks shy as grass.

Meanwhile the river
slides with their ghosts to the sea,
sheet after sheet, each brighter than the last
as the sky opens a vein of pure copper.

On the near side
uncertain with crickets,
smells of grass tangle in my nose,
a chill climbs from the shallows
up the hairs of my arm,
and the small torpedo of the frog
hits the water.

Still, while mist rises,
quietly attentive,
and places damp hands on my forehead,
I would dig my heel in to leave
a sharp imprint,
I would say something, a word
fraying at the edges like a star.

Simple Simon

Now he wags his head, now beats the floor,
out of time with all the dignity,
pomp, and music in this service of our Lord,
this tread and pause of elders steady as trees.
Constrained inside his head all leaps and pushes
to a blur of light, to a hugger-mugger joy,
as if a wind would take each hand and rush
him birdlike to the altar with a cry.

We see his ungainly shadow, not
what his soul by its sharp hunger proves—
that we are fickle with our faculties
and by our spastic wills evade our love—
unlike this simple child whose spirit easily
outstrips where angels groan and dare not.

CHRISTMAS EVE

While cattle stupidly stare
over straw damp from their breathing
and the horse lazily stirs
over his trough, and the lantern
licks at shadows in corners,

in the woods the wild ones gather,
the rabbit twitching with care,
sooty shrew, and imperial mole
with the hands of a lost politician,
to shine in the branch-broken light

of a moon which in mid-career
lights up a church of snow.
Now one paw after another
about the bones of weeds
in a soft worrying circle

the helpless ones dance out their fear,
watching the glittering air
where he shines in the eyes of the others
naked, with nothing to wear.
Long before he comes to the stable

to the shrew's moving smudge on the snow
to the mole's ineffectual gesture
to the soft hide of the hare
he comes, warming each creature
naked in the fangs of the year.

PEONIES

With names like Bleeding Heart and Duchess Slipper
they rose in great heaps on the wagon
as I crouched and cut the stems and crouched again
rhythmically to keep up with the tractor—
the black earth sweet and clinging to my shoes,
the Mexicans' speech about me like a necklace.

The smell of each one nodding against my cheek
as I stooped to pick it, the flush armfuls
of Michigan Beauties landing on the wagon
with a soft hush—cream, white, crimson,
and peach flecked with mauve or carmine—
such clumsy stooping to stand up in a heaven

of perfume and rapidly rising banks of flowers!
Soon my legs cramped and my shirt soaked through
from the wet petals. In rare five-minute breathers
the others smoked and laughed at the greenhorn
whose arms for the first time ached from lifting flowers,
who sat there stunned as from some shameful excess.

Soon the tractor started again and the load trembled.
We had less than an hour to get them to the cooler.
There girls in loose smocks stripped and packed them
in green paper to be flown out that evening
to weddings, banquets, and graduations,
where other girls, gathering in dresses,

would pause long enough for a picture
against the Virginia Dares, the Forever Yours,
the Carolina Mornings. While, back in the welcome cooler,
our wagon empty, our fingers sore from knives,
we'd stand about breathing the cold fragrance
crowding upon our brains like a dark music.

SHOPPING TOGETHER

Cardboard stars crowd the shelves,
and moons marked off a penny,
as you glide, standing on the cart,

to a touch in any direction.
We shine in a dusk of eggplants,
sleepy with a perfume of apples,

wander forests of asparagus,
drift a green ocean
of lettuce, avocados, celery,

down an avalanche of oranges
to a wilderness of bananas—
an El Dorado of lavish aromas.

Still, beyond the parsley are berries
superfluous with juice
that break in our mouths like old sorrows,

and melons like a school of whales
shouldering a cool secret
over the edge of the world.

Last, as we count up our treasures
the register sings and the basket
bumps to the car with your laughter.

Once inside, all the way home,
bags leaning lovesick against us,
ice creams thawing in secret,
we feed each other plums and dark cherries.

Let this day's air praise the Lord—
Rinsed with gold, endless, walking the fields,
Blue and bearing the clouds like censers,
Holding the sun like a single note
Running through all things, a *basso profundo*
Rousing the birds to an endless chorus.

Let the river throw itself down before him,
The rapids laugh and flash with his praise,
Let the lake tremble about its edges
And gather itself in one clear thought
To mirror the heavens and the reckless gulls
That swoop and rise on its glittering shores.

Let the lawn burn continually before him
A green flame, and the tree's shadow
Sweep over it like the baton of a conductor,
Let winds hug the housecorners and woodsmoke
Sweeten the world with her invisible dress,
Let the cricket wind his heartspring
And draw the night by like a child's toy.

Let the tree stand and thoughtfully consider
His presence as its leaves dip and row
The long sea of winds, as sun and moon
Unfurl and decline like contending flags.

Let blackbirds quick as knives praise the Lord,
Let the sparrow line the moon for her nest
And pick the early sun for her cherry,
Let her slide on the outgoing breath of evening,
Telling of raven and dove,
The quick flutters, homings to the green houses.

Let the worm climb a winding stair,
Let the mole offer no sad explanation
As he paddles aside the dark from his nose,
Let the dog tug on the leash of his bark,
The startled cat electrically hiss,
And the snake sign her name in the dust

In joy. For it is he who underlies
The rock from its liquid foundation,
The sharp contraries of the giddy atom,
The unimaginable curve of space,
Time pulling like a patient string,
And gravity, fiercest of natural loves.

At his laughter, splendor riddles the night,
Galaxies swarm from a secret hive,
Mountains split and crawl for aeons
To huddle again, and planets melt
In the last tantrum of a dying star.

At his least signal spring shifts
Its green patina over half the earth,
Deserts whisper themselves over cities,
Polar caps widen and wither like flowers.

In his stillness rock shifts, root probes,
The spider tenses her geometrical ego,
The larva dreams in the heart of the peachwood,
The child's pencil makes a shaky line,
The dog sighs and settles deeper,
And a smile takes hold like the feet of a bird.

Sit straight, let the air ride down your backbone,
Let your lungs unfold like a field of roses,
Your eyes hang the sun and moon between them,
Your hands weigh the sky in even balance,
Your tongue, swiftest of members, release a word
Spoken at conception to the sanctum of genes,
And each breath rise sinuous with praise.

Let your feet move to the rhythm of your pulse
(Your joints like pearls and rubies he has hidden),
And your hands float high on the tide of your feelings.
Now, shout from the stomach, hoarse with music,
Give gladness and joy back to the Lord,
Who, sly as a milkweed, takes root in your heart.

FROM *The Beasts & the Elders*

GETTYSBURG: THE WHEATFIELD

The wheat is swimming toward the sun
in the utter gale of Pennsylvania,
picking the light of stones and pushing
cataracts of trees over the hills.
I see the spotless blue sky swept
clean by the hurrying fields, think of
beards matted with sweat and pollen,
oozing cherry, sour apple, hoarse cries—
the bee dizzily searching for the smashed hive.

"I heard a buzzing sound that stopped.
He took another step and kind of withered.
Funny how he took that step—his hand
went up as if to brush away a fly."

I hear only what I've read
in *American Heritage*, the centennial histories,
voices that scrawl over the years
like the blue smoke from wood-lots,
or drop with loose-jointed ease
like chips from an axe before the furious
tree pulls the sky on the clearing,
and see what I have brought to see,
slickly embalmed from the Brady photos,
to frame with empty trees and fences—

officers baggy around a tilting table,
men leaning against the hind-end of a howitzer
or twisted in the grass, mouths cocked open,
ravenous for flies.

Yet all of this seems hardly plausible
among the dusty grass continually scratching
itself. The creases in my tourist map have
worn through several strategic positions.

In my car again, driving west,
I think of the druids,
whose wicker victims whistled through the fire—
how each year the yellow harvest
climbed wave after wave upon the burning
until, the granaries full, the chieftains fat,
the site was cleaned up for the tourists.
At Auschwitz one reads with mild surprise
the oven-manufacturer's name
stamped on his ware—the baker's hands are
immaculate, white with flour. For a moment
the sun stops. The West swells
around the clot, seeps
through trees. . . .

For two weeks afterward at night
you could see the manes of fires
riding over the treetops, splitting
the horses' teeth, melting their hooves,
until wet with the dawn their clean ribcages,
curved like the hulls of decaying arks,
floated empty over the fields.

for Lee & John Fink

162

AIR FIELD

All day the great planes gingerly descend
an invisible staircase, holding up
their skirts and dignity like great ladies
in technicolor histories, or reascend,
their noses needling upward like a compass
into a wild blue vacuum,
leaving everything in confusion behind:

In some such self-deceiving light as this
we'll view the air force base when moved away
from where its sleepless eye revolves all night.
We'll smile and recollect it conversationally—
tell with what ease the silver planes dropped down
or how they, weightless, rose above
our roof. We'll pass it with the sugar and cream,

forever sheltered from this moment's sick
surprise that we have lived with terror, with pride,
the wounded god circling the globe, never resting,
that in the morning and the evening we have heard
his cry, have seen him drag his silver wings
whining with anguish like a huge
fly seeking to lay its deadly eggs.

Found out in left hayfield
under a crooked moon
bought in a green bottle
in a back alley in Wales
plucked from a rock
where the sea goes rabid—
at night the pink feet
wizen to little hooves.

The transparent extra lid
the elastic web hidden
between silken fingers
in a red wool mitten
or the nibbed horn buried
in a field wild with curls—
may be trimmed at six
burned away like a wart

Though his violet irises
be put under glass
in a symmetrical frame
arranged for at school—
dangerous in adolescence
liable under the moon
to be changed to an elm
married to tulips.

Holds the earth like a marble
between finger and thumb
breathes through grasses
belches clouds
sprouts words like pimples
hoards his shame
evokes a sly lip
from a name.

Grown glues his feet
under the stars
holds his mind inside out
like a Klein jar
up to the world maybe—
maybe not—
his clothes hung about him
like an afterthought.

Farming the yellow squares he learned a rage
for wheat like the sun stooping red-faced over the field,
for hogs anchoring a cloud of dust by the trough,

barns fat with summer, a tractor's shining cleats,
and lilacs muffling the house in a burning cloud.
He learned his way about land, machinery, men,

tilled, repaired, talked, bought and sold
early and late, then drove his Plymouth off the road
when work rose up to take its share of him.

Two heart attacks later I knew his easy walk
across the porch where the screen door yawned
as it swung wide on the cindered street:

his retired black shoes made a comfortable squeak
as if the earth liked his weight upon it.
Outside the ice cream parlor yellow hats

stirred the moist air. Cold orangeade sweated
as, clearing the gravel from his throat, he paused
listening to the whine of the single cooler.

Mornings he'd take me early to fish
for the green catfish I played with on the bank,
trapping in pools till the little dykes gave way—

or ignored entirely to hurt him with my book,
asserting my independence. When he died,
swinging a tailgate shut behind some new calves,

I recalled the way his dentures clicked
cracking strawberry seeds, the morning light
flooding the cantaloupe he cut for me in cubes.

A Bear

A white bear groped the orchard of my dream,
Gulped cherries down his inexact raw throat,
His paws were bleeding blindly and his muzzle,
Sweet cherry, sweet cherry, sweet cherry—

                        I shot
The huge blind bear so enormously stuffing
Himself with winds of flowers, heaps of grass-
Green partridges, red and yellow marmosets,

And down he came with the bread of heaven
Thunderous on my brazen coat. I deferred
Handshakes and all grave bear solemnities,
Touching his wounded eyes and ears and nose.

He sang a slow song as he smoothly died,
Lifting his nose to the east and to the west,
A thin and quavering note for so large a beast
That crept in a slow stain across my vest.

Then blazing like a furnace of white snow
He lifted cavernous wings and drew
To his full height—his blood hung in bright beads—
He flexed his feathers once and flew

In a flattering arc to the sun that swelled
Imperceptibly to drink him in, then shone
As usual. Each day it's shone the same
Since I first rubbed my eyes to find him gone.

SNAKESONG

In the green swim of trees
in the silk clothes of spring
when sparse birds
made a singing net
and small red barks

split at the green nudge
I clung to the trunks
went under the roots
to the heart of the pull
sidled, rustled

sloughed off my skin
and waved my word
thin red fire
around the spotted
and dewed damps of life

small numps
uncurling
twigs ticking and swelling
flames of newts
rabbits in scuds

puffing like milkweed.
I curled round the garden
thin hose of breath
noose of the spirit
simple string

undone by everything.
Such I was
before I walked a man
or made palaver
or wavered at woman

before that sweet fig
fixed my tooth
and, scotched, I sagged
to the cellar of roots
and coiling thought

soon with feet and hands
to cling to the sky
move upright as a tree
in the crooked light
find my tongue and spread
a mist over the world.

NUDE

Content in her skin she does not challenge
the blue shadow cast over most of her body,
waiting in the shade like a center of gravity,
so full, even the trees have travelled too far.

Her breasts steal the wind with surprise,
promise long savannahs of discovery
beyond the trembling compass of a flower
or tuft of weeds agog with her sweet breath.

I stand in this museum looking,
blood sagging to my fingers and toes.
The sun is coming at me through the wall.
Clothes could never touch her, this one, put
beyond the night whisper and morning's flat red mouth
into the first turning of the light.

Ribithoids, by Macrowcz, 073.869.10-6A, written on a
slip of paper floating between fingers before him
to the narrow door, hedged in stone,
the same stone shelving out over,
under, eons of books compressed into
ten levels, wedged in steel vertebrae,
ganglia for the enormous brain that sheds
a little light out these windows—once
John Harvard's few shelves, now plunging
stories into the earth.

                              Going down
from Level 4 to Level 3, from American
to English literature, oppressed
by the millions of cells thinking
in the darkness between covers,
the word buried in the pulp of trees.
Down to Sub-level B. Stairs clang: up the
square mouth a soft meadowy thing in a sweater,
books pressed quivering to her, cloud
of flowers, momentary. Then that staid
smell of old authors shrinking in the cellar,
distant seed of the tree of knowledge
more elusive for its sextillion sprouts,
steady and shrewd scent of worlds
never to be cracked. Down
to Sub-level D. The slip is pale
against the blue fluorescent damp—
potable stone.

Ribithoids, by Macrowcz, an unintelligible title
by an unpronounceable author—reason enough:
This is the book to break that
chain of looking up to add
to what one knows, which always leads to
looking up something else. Bald-headed man asleep on
the second, third, and eighth volumes
of Crabbits' *Dictionary of the Visigoths*. The
radiator clucks like a brooding hen.

This is the book to give the secret
whole—the isolate knowledge, ethereal
and complete, in whose faintest iota swims
the luminous gnat-swarm of the worlds.
This is the fruit whose pierced skin
froths with stars, at whose succulent word
the snake swallows his tail into light.
This is the fruit of that forbidden tree
whose roots crawl over maps and faces,
sink through this cellar nine
times all of relative space to the center.

He moves along the last aisle, bulb burnt out,
lighting a match over the backward books—
Ribwort, Ribs—then nothing but solid
wall one inch away from Macrowcz 10 6A
buried in stone!

The snake's skeleton rattles through the pipes.
The gleaming-headed sleeper after knowledge
snores. Back to Coleridge and Lowes'
Road to Xanadu, where he who pauses to pluck
a footnote is lost. Back to the link
that is not missing, back to Coleridge and
opium, the regulated stall, books
to check in and books to check out.

The root goes too deep.

In a Farmhouse Near Porlock

In the summer of the year 1797, the author,
then in ill health, had retired to a lonely
farmhouse between Porlock and Linton. . . .
—Coleridge's Introduction to "Kubla Khan"

At home in her kitchen wife Sara grieves:
The tiles are unmended, the shoe money gone.
When she poured boiling milk on that abstracted form,
It had smiled and written a three-shilling poem.*

In a farmhouse near Porlock Coleridge sleeps
As the red noon licks itself to a ball.
A Collector from Porlock knocks loud through the hall:
Is anyone here, anybody at all?

By a farmhouse near Porlock a frayed moon sings
Like the bitter half of a wedding ring.
Huge blocks of night beat on the wall
And a tree shakes the green pulse of a star:
Nobody here, nobody at all!

In a farmhouse near Porlock sun and moon walk
Like red and silvery crabs on the sand,
Cold hand in hot where the heavens crack white,
And a head splits wide at the edge of a voice:
Is anyone, anyone here at all?

And there in the midst of the whirligig
Light put its stick and broke the string,
Night hooted by on its rickety rails,
The garden sprung, the day shook free,

All space snaked by and a mind floated blithe
As a bubble on a column of breath,
The lion rolled out his red-carpeted tongue,
Lambs leaped in the green fields of his breath.

Then the fist fell like a cindered star.
The door licked dry lips, the lid snapped down.
A Man a Man a Man from the Town!—
A shoestring was broken, the fire out—
"Here I am! Lord! Here I am!"
And Coleridge went out.

for Robert Barth

*An earlier poem, "This Lime-Tree Bower My Prison,"
written after the recounted accident
prevented Coleridge from going on a walk with
William and Dorothy Wordsworth and Charles Lamb.*

VOICE OF MANY WATERS

To him that overcometh will I give to eat of the hidden manna,
and will give him a white stone, and in the stone a new name
written, which no man knoweth saving he that receiveth it.

The night is cluttered with stars.
   The drift of the earth
is dark, enormous
   bulking shoulder of the undersea whale
in the Atlantic's winking canyons.
   Trees wait
for the slow stain of day
   walking now over the water
west of England.

   I put two sticks on the fire
on the ghost of logs
   that fade into the red eye
drawing the circle of my campsite
   about which hang
my all-weather tent, glinting axe
   myself, like planets
inching the swarm of stars.

Twelve o'clock:
The beast startles first with his foot
    broad as unbearable moon,
his leg the shank of stars
    his mane the black roar of space
turning to the white heart of fire
    in which begin to move
thick and uncertain

    the rivery shapes of trees
bending over water
    cradling a platinum light
running to gold
    and pebbles
each speckled with suns
    each turned and lapped by the water.

Green steals over me:
    I am swung in a net of leaves.
Birds wrap me tight in their songs:
    drunk with the trauma of flowers
I am and I hear a voice calling
    within the voices of water.
A shadow brightens the ground.
    A hand darkens all but itself.

Somewhere in the face of the trees
    a large clumsy beast is singing
the brood of pain and music
    played on the stops of the worlds
the flute of starlight and vacuum
    the unending theme of Abyss
and the trees are growing before me
    translating all to flowers.

Now the voice is within a white stone
    round in my hand like water
that speaks one word running through fingers
    to shred in my mouth like the moon.
Outside the sun is rising. Blue,
    the sky is blue
and the far forest neighing.

    I wake in the orange flower of my tent.

for Clyde Kilby

About Paraclete Press

Who We Are

Paraclete Press is an ecumenical publisher of books on Christian spirituality for people of all denominations and backgrounds.

We publish books that represent the wide spectrum of Christian belief and practice—Catholic, Orthodox, and Protestant.

We market our books primarily through booksellers; we are what is called a "trade" publisher, which means that we like it best when readers buy our books from booksellers, our partners in successfully reaching as wide an audience as possible.

Paraclete Press is the publishing arm of The Community of Jesus, an ecumenical monastic community in the Benedictine tradition. We are uniquely positioned in the marketplace without connection to a large corporation or conglomerate and with informal relationships to many branches and denominations of faith. We focus on publishing a diversity of thoughts and perspectives—the fruit of our diversity as a company.

What We Are Doing

Paraclete Press is publishing books that show the diversity and depth of what it means to be Christian. We publish books that reflect the Christian experience across many cultures, time periods, and houses of worship.

We publish books about spiritual practice, history, ideas, customs, and rituals, and books that nourish the vibrant life of the church.

We have several different series of books within Paraclete Press, including the bestselling Living Library series of modernized classic texts, A Voice from the Monastery—giving voice to men and women monastics on what it means to live a spiritual life today, and Many Mansions—for exploring the riches of the world's religious traditions and discovering how other faiths inform Christian thought and practice.

Learn more about us at our Web site:
www.paracletepress.com, or call us toll-free at
1-800-451-5006.